Justice is Blonde

The Unorthodox Story of an Orthodox Woman

Hon. Lee B. First

Book by Judge Lee Blech First
Updated by Gabi Stefansky
Contact at 646.946.9904 / 646.944.5229
Copyright © 2023 by Lee B. First

Table of Contents

Life in Switzerland..12
We Escape to America..20
My Education and Americanization........................25
Love Struck Home...30
The Life of Handsome Harry...................................35
Religious Transformation of Handsome Harry.......48
Our Wedding Takes Place.......................................53
I Combine Career with a Family.............................59
How to Get a Maid and Keep Her..........................66
Parenting with Pleasure..69
Seth and Shari Find Mates.....................................77
Shari's Wedding, Lubavitch Style...........................80
Mitchell Finds a Bride...83
Celebrating My Anniversaries................................87
Let's Go To My Parties..96
I Love To Decorate..106
I Become a Judge..110
Some Of My Interesting Cases.............................114
Long Distance Parenting......................................118
Comments on Israel..123
Our Foothold In Israel...126
My 50th Wedding Anniversary.............................129
Conclusion...135
Summation of Judge Gorgeous Today................. 139
Some of my Favorite Instagrams......................... 140
A Tribute to Harry First...143

This book is dedicated to my
Beloved Husband
Children
And Grandchildren

I would like to thank Gabi Stefansky for the great contribution he has made to my life and to this book.

Although the original version of this book has been written years ago, it has been updated with much new material. Because history should be kept alive, most of this book has remained as the original one, while new parts of my life have been added. I hope you enjoy my GORGEOUS story.

Lee B. First

CHAPTER 1
LIFE IN SWITZERLAND

Two facts you would never guess from looking at me: one, I'm an observant Jew and two, I'm a judge. My long blond ringlets and dynamic way of dressing have won me the nickname "Judge Gorgeous." The hair is a wig, though, and my clingy outfits all cover the knees and elbows because we strictly orthodox women are to be modest.

My friend claims to have a more fitting label for my brand of traditional Judaism. She says that because of my openness, theme parties, and penchant for telling lively jokes, I'm really "Cheerydox."

It is a struggle to remain low key and avoid bragging sometimes, especially about my main man, Handsome Harry, whom I would never have met had I been quiet and reserved. But more of that later. This is supposed to be my life story, so let's go back to earlier times.

As a child, I could see the snow-capped Alps from my window. But I had other peaks and valleys to contend with in my native Zurich, namely school life. Learning came easily to me, and I truly loved my classes. But whenever the teacher announced a test, we kids responded as expected. I had my private reason for groaning.

We attended school six days a week (half days on Wednesdays and Saturdays.) Since Orthodox Jews aren't allowed to carry anything on the Sabbath, my parents paid a classmate to carry my books to and from school. For some reason, the teachers always chose to give us tests on days I couldn't write, and for writing there could be no stand-ins.

Because Mr. Gruber had a pleasant face, I was encouraged to ask if I could please have the test on a different day since my religion prevented me from writing on Saturday.

"That is too bad for you, then, isn't it dear?" he said softly.

I was crushed. I felt myself turning red, but managed to hold back my tears until I got home. Seeing how upset I was, Mama offered to speak to the teacher. This was great news because Mama impressed everyone she met. She was a beautiful woman who took pride in her appearance. In her modish wig and smart clothes, she looked elegant. Her carriage was regal, as befit the daughter of Rabbi Mordechai Shor of Poland and the wife of Rabbi Ben Zion Blech of Switzerland.

Eagerly, I awaited her return, confident that I would be able to take my test with my fellow classmates. I'd do well and make them all proud of me-Papa, Mama, my brothers Sammy and Benny, Grandma, Grandpa, and all my aunts, uncles, and cousins that lived upstairs. When I heard her steps, I flew to the door.

Mama sighed; her eyes looked tired.

"It's no use," she said. "The teacher says he will never change the day just to suit us Jews, and that his main concern happens to be educating the children of Swiss citizens."

"Swiss citizens," Papa echoed. "The only way to gain that status is by having Swiss parents."

That triggered an old hurt of mine. "Is that why they keep calling me an 'Auslander' (foreigner), even though I was born right here in Zurich?" I asked.

Papa smiled his bittersweet smile. "Don't worry," he said. "Anti-Semitism is not new to our people, and it's not new to this family. We managed to survive before and we will find a way around it again."

That night I couldn't sleep. I tip-toed to the kitchen and listened by the door while Mama and Papa spoke in serious tones over their hot chocolate.

"How about buying a regular suit now?" she asked.

I had heard that question before and I knew exactly what she meant. Both my parents had been born in Poland. When my father was three years old, his family emigrated to Austria where he and his five brothers and sisters were raised. Unlike other Viennese Jews, his family retained the traditional Chassidic garb of the "shtetl" (small town). When poverty forced him to take a job outside the country, he refused to blend in like the other German-speaking Jews of Switzerland.[1]

"Never!" said Papa. "My beard, my black hat and coat- these are how I identify with my heritage, and how I keep reminding myself who I am." You know, it is written in the Bible that after Adam ate the fruit that Eve gave him, he realized he was naked and hid himself. So G-d called out, 'Where are you, Adam?' Now since G-d is all knowing, why did he have to ask that question? He was really asking, 'Where are you, the real you Adam?' From this we learn that when a person dies and comes before the Heavenly Judge he will not be asked 'Why were you not like Moses in your deeds?' or 'Why were you not brilliant like

---

[1] Incidentally, these particular Jews are still called "Yeckies" by some, from the word "Jacke," a short, suit-type jacket.

Maimonides?' No, G-d will ask only, 'Why were you not like yourself? Where was the true you?' Well, the true me is a Jew, and I'm proud enough to let the world know it. Mama was silent for a moment. "But if the officials here could not tell right away that you are Jewish," she said, "then you could apply for citizenship and pass the interview as well as the test. That way we might all..."

"And what about the Swiss jargon that I don't speak? A person could easily break his tongue over that language... Anyway, who knows how long we'll be here? The rumor is that Hitler is planning to invade Switzerland. And you know what that means..."

I shuddered. In 1938, Hitler's armies had marched into Vienna, and horrible things were done to the Jews. When Papa heard that they were being made to scrub the streets with a toothbrush while Nazi soldiers urinated on them, he rushed to the border and carried both his mother and father over the mountains. This was no mean feat, given the fact that my grandmother was dying of diabetes and my grandfather was severely crippled. His slow, shuffling walk dated back to the time when he deliberately injured himself in order to avoid having to serve in the anti-Semitic Austrian Army.[2]

I remember visiting them in Austria when I was about three or four years old and being struck by their poverty. Since there were not enough beds for all the children, chairs were lined up every night to be slept on.

---

[2] An interesting sidelight is that his family found him a wife even though he was unable to work. How did they manage? While he took care of the children at home, my grandmother supported the family as a traveling saleswoman. Thus, my liberated streak goes back pretty far.

We had also visited my Polish grandparents in a small hut where they had raised nine children. I realize now that ours was just a lower middle-class family, but compared to what I saw there, I thought we were millionaires. Instead of pavement, a muddy path ran in front of their house; the pigs walked freely down the main street. I had never seen an outhouse before and I am told I did my best to avoid using it.

Going to "shul" (synagogue) with my grandfather left an indelible mark on me. I was used to the cold, serious prayer style of the German-Jews, and the swaying and wailing I now witnessed moved me deeply. I ran up to several people and tugged at their clothes. "Don't cry, don't cry," I begged. "G-d will bring you better days."

On a physical basis, our life in Switzerland was very comfortable. We lived in a five room apartment and were lucky it was situated on top of a bar, since this was the only place with a telephone in the vicinity (although we did have to be entertained by loud music way into the night). I always remembered how I feared for my father (who wore a Prince Albert, sidelocks and reddish blond beard) when I saw him going to answer the phone in the bar filled with drunken, singing Swiss-who have never been known for their love of foreigners.

Because there were about 10.000 Jews in Switzerland in those days, there were numerous synagogues, most of them Orthodox, yet there was no Jewish day school in Zurich, or any other major city. All of us were compelled to attend public schools and an afternoon Hebrew school that was attended by both boys and girls. There was, however, one Jewish day school (yeshiva) for boys in Montreux, which attracted students from all over Europe. There was also a wonderful Jewish boarding school in Bex-les-Bains, known as Ascher, run by Dr. Simon Ascher and his family, to which many wealthy Jews from all over the world sent their children.

In the summer we went to summer camp for three weeks, since, unlike America, we did not have a two-month long summer vacation. The name of the camp was Heiden, but it was more a prison camp than a vacation place. Although the camp was beautifully situated in the mountains, it was run strictly according to Swiss rules. No waste was allowed. I shall never forget that, at lunch, if we did not eat something we despised (as children are wont to do), the same food was brought to us for supper. We were forced to consume what was served, regardless. In the late 1930's the Jewish community of Switzerland raised funds to keep the camp open. Many hundreds of children who escaped the Nazis were sent there by their parents until other arrangements could be made for them. I can still see the tears shed by these children crying for their parents, most of whom they probably never saw again.

My two brothers and I always dressed in strictly Swiss attire. I wore a "dirndle" with an apron (a flower print dress native to Switzerland and the Austrian Tyrol), a white bow in my hair, and white knee socks-all of which I shed on my first day in America. My brothers wore "lederhosen" (leather shorts) and Swiss skullcaps, known as "sanechapli." These skullcaps were commonly worn in the Alps by men and boys. As Jews, my brothers normally wore skullcaps, so this Swiss garb prevented them from being distinguished as Jews and, as such, lessened any potential anti-Semitism.

Although Switzerland was one of the more advanced nations in Europe, we still did not have central heating. There was a tile stove in each of our rooms which had to be stoked with coal. This was delivered regularly to our home and left in a bin in our basement. We, of course, were not wealthy enough to heat all our rooms, and I'll never forget how, as a child, I never wanted to go to bed for fear that I would freeze to death. Generally, one hour before we went to bed, we would place our feather bed covers on the tile stove and heat them up, so that when we finally made it through the cold bedroom we could jump into a warm bed.

Taking on the job of assistant Rabbi and shochet (ritual slaughterer for kosher meat) in Zurich made Papa the richest in the family. He sent money not only to his parents, but to other members of the family as well. Besides his parents, he also brought over his two brothers and one sister, with their families. We rented another apartment on the top floor of our building and they all moved in. We regularly had 28 diners sitting at our table. I loved being surrounded by all these loving cousins, aunts, and uncles, but my joy was short-lived.

Since the Swiss did not take kindly to refugees, it was arranged for all of my father's relatives to leave for America. His sister, however, had been introduced to a scholarly rabbi and their subsequent marriage allowed her to remain with us. Because my grandmother had just died, my grandfather also chose to stay with us-he adored my mother who took fabulous care of him.

Now the rumors of an impending invasion grew hotter. One day Hitler's armies were said to be invading from the east, the next day from the north. Time to make a decision: we would lock up our beloved home, pack a few belongings, and wait near the Swiss border. Thank G-d the Nazi's never did overrun Switzerland. I understand, though, that the country was full of German officers and that plans for a concentration camp in Davos had been laid out. My own feeling is that Hitler would have been welcomed with open arms by the Swiss, just as they were by the Austrians.

By 1941, we had had enough. My father got a job as a rabbi in New York, and we stateless ones were now on our way to America.

Making that move proved to be nowhere as easy as it sounds.

CHAPTER 2
WE ESCAPE TO AMERICA

When I compare traveling from Switzerland to America today with the ordeal we went through, it's as though we were coming from another planet.

Our journey from the little border town we had gone to from our Swiss home took us first through unoccupied France. I still have strong memories of literally wall-to-wall people on that horrendous train ride. Every inch of the floor and the overhead luggage rack was packed with desperate humanity. There was absolutely no food on board, and whenever the train ground to a halt at the station, there would be a mad scramble to buy something to eat or drink.

German officers were everywhere. Their uniforms alone were enough to scare us. We did not yet know the atrocities these men were capable of. What little we heard, we could not bring ourselves to believe.

The next lap of our trip sounded very exciting to my young ears. We had tickets for a Spanish ship which would shortly be taking us across the Atlantic to the U.S.A. We arrived in Barcelona in the middle of the night. Talk about culture shock. The city was all lit up; hordes of refugees roamed the crowded streets. It was quite a contrast to our quiet, little Switzerland where policemen drove down the streets nightly at seven, sounding a bell to signal that it was closing time for shopkeepers.

We went on to Madrid, and from there to the seaport of Cadiz. To our great disappointment, no ship was in sight. It was then we learned that the real meaning of manana was not "tomorrow," but more closely, "someday." The tomorrows turned into several months.

By this time, HIAS (the Hebrew Immigrant Aid Society) had brought in more people to await the ship.

We all stayed together at the same, local, beautiful hotels. Each was built around a local courtyard where musicians played as we dined.

Food was in short supply. I still recall the dark pan that tasted more like cardboard than bread to me. And I'm still haunted by the many pairs of eyes that we could see staring at us through cracks in the walls, watching every morsel we put in our mouths.

Spain was then suffering the results of the recent Civil War- loss of lives, diminished food supply, and a poor economy. As we walked through the streets, we were like the Pied Piper of Hamelin with hundreds of beggars following us. Hard though it was, we tried to share what we could.

Finally, the long awaited vessel arrived, a freighter called the Navemar. We had paid $500 apiece, a fortune in those days, for accommodations that proved to be nonexistent. With over a thousand people clamoring to get on board, those in charge decided to let their greed override their compassion.

They gutted the inside of the ship, cramming it with bunk- beds-500 of them in one room for the male

passengers and 500 in another for the women. Health conditions were terrible. There was hardly any water, and it was impossible to wash. Because of the poor refrigeration, food spoilage caused illness and even death.

After a couple of days we reached Lisbon. My father and several other observant Jews got off and bought fruit, fish, vegetables, some pots and pans. Now, at least, we had our own little kitchen onboard, one that was comparatively clean and safe.

Then trouble struck our family. My poor father contracted typhoid fever. Despite his severe illness, he remained in the same room with the rest of the men. A doctor who admired my father took care of him as best as he could, given the shortage of medical supplies.

Many passengers slept on the decks or in lifeboats in order to avoid the crowded quarters below. There was a good deal of illness, and our numbers dwindled every night, as the bodies of those who died were thrown overboard.

Despite all these hardships, there was music and singing on the ship. Together with all the grim lessons, I also learned that in the midst of trouble, life went on. People fell in love, and I'd see them talking and laughing at night. The prevailing mood was one of joy because, after all, they had just escaped certain destruction and were now on their way to freedom.

One day, after more than three weeks, the word went reverberating around the freighter: "We're here! We're in America!" Everybody rushed on deck, and there she was: the Statue of Liberty!

My father would not see this vision with us because he had been taken off the ship and hospitalized when we docked in Cuba. My mother now arrived in a new land with her three little ones and her ailing father-in-law, not knowing when and if she'd ever see her husband again.

Word about the Navemar had preceded our arrival. "Hell Ship Arrives!" the headlines screamed. Not only was there a swarm of reporters around (already I was famous!), there were a good many lawyers as well. It seems the bar had heard: a) how much we had paid for our fare, and b) how badly we had been mistreated.

Their eagerness to right that wrong for us was intense. And, since those were hard times for the legal profession, the prospect of handling 500 cases in one shot was not exactly one they wanted to overlook.

Upon disembarking, we faced a reception committee made up of the press, immigration people, and lawyers with retainers. (By the way, we eventually did recover most of our passage money.)

We arrived on Friday towards evening, and stood by the gangplank perplexed. It was close to the onset of the Sabbath when we were not permitted to travel. What a dilemma! Luckily, a taxi came by and quickly got us to the Boro Park, Brooklyn address where our relatives had settled.

Our first impression of that borough was of beauty beyond our wildest dreams. Not one, but hundreds of trees grew in Brooklyn. My aunt lived in a two-family house with a beautiful garden. To me it seemed like paradise.

Unfortunately, my father would not be able to join us for several months. His father, on the other hand, had shlepped with us all those miles through war-torn Europe, as he chose to stay with us.

Grandfather Blech was a handsome man with blond hair and blue eyes. He had a great love of beautiful things and beautiful people. Part of the reason he enjoyed living with our family was that my mother always looked like a Hollywood movie star. It was also fun having him around. Every time my mother returned from going out, we all knew exactly what he would say.

"Well? How many men killed themselves today because they couldn't have you?"

I think I take after him. I also have a great love for beautiful people, as you will see pretty soon when I get to the part about "Handsome Harry."

Our first day in America brought a wonderful surprise. Not only had our family found and rented an apartment for us in Boro Park, they had also completely decorated it and even stocked it with food. It was a fine start for the new life that we faced in our new land.

CHAPTER 3
MY EDUCATION AND AMERICANIZATION

When I first arrived on these shores in 1941, I couldn't speak a word of English. I was lucky, though, to have the world's greatest teachers-Cary Grant, Greer Garson, Spencer Tracy, and Katharine Hepburn among others.

As it happened, I was twice blessed. The approach taken by my school principal at the time also made a lot of sense. Today, when people want my views on bilingual education, I must be frank. While I would very much like to help newcomers adjust to our country, I question how wise it is to provide them with classes in their native language. My own experience is what makes me wonder.

When I entered seventh grade at Montauk Junior High School, the principal did not throw me into the regular departmental system. It's true that I moved from class to class as the others did, but while they went from English to math to history, I went from English 7 to English 8 to English 9-nothing but English classes all day long.

At first, I just sat there and listened, bewildered; then, very gradually, I began to take part. After about six weeks of attending these classes, going to the movies, and just hearing English spoken everywhere but at home, I acquired a fairly good command of the language.

By the time the spring semester rolled around, I was ready for the regular eighth grade program. Not only did I find myself able to keep up, but I also even managed to get very high grades in all my subjects. Would you believe I actually won a couple of spelling bees?

We spoke German at home, and in order to communicate with the rest of the family, I now easily picked up Yiddish. In Zurich, we had never dared speak Yiddish in public, and my parents always spoke German to us and to each other. There was quite a bit of anti-Semitism around, so we really can't fault the Jews of that time for wanting to avoid standing out by their garb or their speech.

Today, it's a new Switzerland. On a recent visit, I was pleasantly surprised to see the streets filled with Chassidic Jews talking away in Yiddish without the slightest trace of self-consciousness. It seems that many of them stayed on after the war, intermarried with the German Jews, and somehow made them proud of their heritage. Some of their children who attended school in Israel came home wearing black hats instead of Swiss caps. In the main "Yecke" shul, the sermons are actually given in Yiddish! We had always been urged to think of ourselves as Swiss citizens first, but today one can be overtly Jewish and a good Swiss citizen as well.

The same sort of embarrassment about the Yiddish tongue prevailed here in the United States in my era. Whenever I spoke that language, someone was sure to call me a "green horn" (a term that was originally used to describe an immature ox with young or "green horns"). There was a general feeling in the land that to converse in a foreign tongue was "un-American" behavior.

Here, too, we have come full circle. When we recently asked my son what qualities he liked about his new fiancée, he said, "She's beautiful, she's smart, she's a good person, and she speaks Yiddish." Obviously, he considered the latter skill a big plus.

Today, I too am glad that I know the language so well. As a judge, I find it wonderful to be able to understand the speech of some of those appearing before me, before the interpreter gets to do his work.

Getting back to my days as a new immigrant, I recall one small incident that filled me with joy. On my third day here we went shopping at Klein's, a clothing store on 14th Street in Manhattan. The policeman who was directing traffic overheard us and told us in Yiddish to be careful crossing. Imagine, a uniformed authority figure who spoke Yiddish! Surely, fate had brought us to the land of our dreams.

As for my religious studies, Boro Park had no "yeshivas" for girls at that time, so I was registered in the public school. When my father recovered from typhoid and arrived here a few months later, he took active measures to round out my education.

Having heard that the Bais Yakov School was about to branch out to Boro Park, he saw to it that I was registered. Thus, I became one of the first students of the local edition of a school system with an interesting history.

Until about 1917, Torah study in Poland was restricted to boys. Girls who wanted an education went to gymnasium, where they pursued secular studies and, in many cases, stopped being observant.

This state of affairs disturbed a Polish Jewish woman named Sarah Schenirer. In a move that might be viewed as women's liberation of her day, she founded the first Bais Yakov school for religious studies for girls in Cracow, Poland. Many of the Rabbis were so outraged by this action, that they put her in cherem (declared her an outcast). Later on a number of rabbis and prominent rebbes began to support her, and that is when the school really took off.

It is one of life's ironies that the institution that was deemed so radical at its start is considered "right wing" today. The branch that I attended in the '40s was above a store on 13th Avenue. It had no English department, and our curriculum was quite different from that of the boys. We studied Chumash (the Bible), but not the halacha (laws) interpreting the five Holy Books. We also learned about permissible and non-permissible behavior, without being taught the reasons or origins thereof. We had to keep our traditions based on faith alone.[3]

Despite these limitations, my father, with his Polish-Austrian background, viewed teaching girls any religious subjects at all as a sign of tremendous progress.

As for my secular education, with America's recent depression firm in everyone's memory, my cousins strongly advised me to take a commercial course at Montauk, in order to prepare myself for the job market.

As it turned out, learning typing and shorthand was one of the wisest moves I ever made. When I later went to college, I could quickly take notes at all the lectures, catching my professors' every word. I'm sure this skill helped account for my excellent grades.

---

[3] This is why when a Jew says his daily prayer, known as the Sh'ma ("Hear Oh Israel, The Lord is Our Lord, The Lord is One"), he must place his hands over his eyes and close them to prove to the world that although we do not see the Lord personally, we still have faith that he exists.

All of these events, of course, took place B.H. What do these letters stand for? I got the idea from a friend that I ran into one day. She recounted an incident that happened in Boro Park.

>"All that happened here B.C.," she said.
>"What's B.C.?" I asked.
>"Before the Chassidim," was her answer.

For me, then, B.H. is "Before Harry," the handsome man who would soon be coming into my life.

CHAPTER 4
LOVE STRUCK HOME

I continued attending Bais Yakov after my classes at New Utrecht High School, where I had switched from the commercial to the academic course. My family had always loved education and, in fact, even had a tradition of women attending college-a highly unusual practice among the religious back then.

My school choices were simple: Brooklyn College, Brooklyn College, or Brooklyn College. No one I knew was applying to an out-of-town school. In the first place, who could afford it? And in the second, which father in our circle would let his daughter out of his sight to that extent?

The truth is, I led a very sheltered life. For example, I was never permitted to go out on dates. My only socializing with young men took the form of shiduchim (matches) that my father brought home for me.

Where did we go? Nowhere. In the old European tradition of my father, a typical "date" went this way: the boy would appear at my house at the appointed time, accompanied by his parents. Over light refreshments in the living room, his folks would interview me. At the same time, my father, to whom religious observance and genealogy were paramount, would be questioning my potential in-laws.

I am reminded of the story where a Chassidic young man comes to be interviewed by his prospective father-in-law. When the girl's father asks him, "How do you propose to support my daughter?" he answers, "G-d will provide." When asked, "Where will you get a car to drive my daughter around?" he answers once again, "G-d will provide." He then leaves, and the prospective father-in-law calls his daughter and tells her that she must marry this young man. The daughter is astonished and asks, "Why?" Her father answers, "HE'S THE ONLY PERSON I KNOW WHO THINKS I'M G-D!"

Actually, with most Jews "too busy making a living to have time for the old traditions." the Orthodox community was small enough for people to be able to check each other out. My parents always saw the candidate as one bound to follow his father's trade or profession. In Europe, after all, the son of a shoemaker became a shoemaker, the son of a rabbi, a rabbi. They didn't realize that in America anyone could reach for the stars.

If the parents didn't hit it off, that was the end of it. The question has been asked: "What is the difference between in-laws and outlaws?" The answer is: "OUTLAWS ARE ALWAYS WANTED!" Fortunately, the fellow and I were also allowed our say. As might be expected, I was never one to need prompting on that score.

"Well, how did you like that one?" Papa would ask after the encounter. "I understand that he is a brilliant Torah scholar."

"But Papa," I'd wail, "he is not at all good-looking!" "Good-looking, rich, and religious-those are the three different matches. You can't have everything, so you'd better decide on one."

Okay, then. He'd narrowed the issue, and I was ready to comply. My choice was good looks. Maybe it's all for the best that I let myself be ruled by feelings rather than logic.

Some of today's young people try to agree upon every last detail in advance, such as where they will live, what schools their children will attend, etc. To my way of thinking, this makes no sense at all. One cannot simply pre-plan one's entire life because things will not turn out that way anyway. Only G-d has the master plan.

That is not to say that I don't admire the way my father lived. While the majority of people went rushing about letting their financial concerns eclipse their spiritual side, my father was different. As a rabbi, he had the time to sit and study for hours every afternoon. I regret that we, his children, never really knew what a great mitzvah (good deed, commandment) he was doing for all of us. Only as adults did we get to understand the belief that in order for the world to continue to exist there must always be someone, somewhere, studying the laws of the Bible. This is the reason the world was created round, so that if it is night in one part of the world, it is day in another and at all times someone is studying our Holy Bible.

We are told that although the laws about visiting the sick, respecting one's parents, etc., are all of great importance, the study of Torah supersedes them all. I guess that the reason is that if we consciously learn what is to be done, then we'll do it. But if we do not learn the right way, then we might observe the laws incorrectly, or not at all. To this day, I try to emulate my father by learning something from the Bible every day.

How do I make time for this very vital activity? Part of the answer might surprise a lot of people, especially those who see me swimming regularly. Little do they suspect that while I am doing my laps, I am also listening intently to tapes made by my brother, Rabbi Benjamin Blech, Spiritual Leader of the Young Israel of Oceanside, New York. I wear a special waterproof pouch that enables me to learn Torah and swim at the same time.

Now for the event that changed my life. At one time, my studies leaned to foreign languages. As a college freshman, I chose that major with the ultimate aim of teaching that subject. One day, I made what I thought was a perfectly logical assumption, namely that I could get some studying done in the Brooklyn College Library.

This proved not to be the case. A unique distraction in the form of a tall, dark, and extremely handsome librarian made it totally impossible for me to concentrate on my work. What was I to do? My smitten 18 year old heart drove me to poetry, and I began to write.

> *My dear young man,*
> *May I confess*
> *That I have desires*
> *I should repress.*
>
> *And you're the one*
> *Who creates them in my heart,*
> *For it is your beauty*
> *That from my studies*
> *makes me part.*
>
> *Innocently I entered*
> *The library tonight*
> *Not wishing to gaze upon An enchanting sight,*

But merely to study
For my final examination.
Yet, as I sat down,
There came temptation.

Temptation to lay my eyes
On your good looks.
Can't resist them;
Can't keep my mind on my books.

And thus I surrender.
To home I am returning.
I have just discovered:
"The library's no longer
a place of learning!"

On my way out, I handed the young man the poem. I knew that I had just experienced a strong, one-sided case of "love at first sight," but I had absolutely no idea what, if anything, would be happening next.

CHAPTER 5
THE LIFE OF HANDSOME HARRY

What happened next? Nothing. Harry First, part-time librarian at Brooklyn College, was also big-man-on-his-block as a returned World War I veteran. A graduate student at Brooklyn Law School, he was used to being approached by girls and hardly noticed the attentions of a mere eighteen-year-old freshman. What had his life been like up to this point? Here's how he tells it:

I was born in the East New York section of Brooklyn and grew up in Brownsville. At home, my parents spoke Yiddish to my brother, my three sisters and me. We made a point of answering them in English. In this way, it worked out that we taught them English while they taught us Yiddish.

The fact is that I was embarrassed when my folks spoke Yiddish in public, and I hated going to the Jewish theater with them. Today, I love the Yiddish stage and I'm proud that I speak the language fluently.

During the 1930's, in that part of Brooklyn, most of the kids in public school were Jewish, and most of the teachers were gentile. Though school was open on such minor religious holidays as Sukkot, most of us stayed home.

When I was growing up, the public school system was far superior to Hebrew schools like the one my parents forced me to attend. These schools, therefore, turned off many of my generation to Jewish education. It's interesting that we hardly lived our heritage, but we never forgot or denied it. Thus, though we were all Bar Mitzvah, we attended shul only on Rosh Hashana and Yom Kippur, or in order to say Kaddish (the prayer for the dead).

It was only many years later, after I had married Lee, that I began to develop a thirst for Jewish education. I was overjoyed to receive the multi-volumed History of the Jews by Gratz as a wedding gift, and am probably one of the few people who ever read the work from cover to cover in one shot.

I was raised with the Jewish work ethic. Two words my parents taught me: gay fardeen (go out and earn). This is completely unlike the boy in the story whose father tells him, "Son, I'm gonna teach you three words. If you learn to say them correctly, you'll never go hungry." "Yeah?" asks the kid. "What are the three words, Pop?" "Stick 'em up!" says the father.

My folks let me smoke, as long as I earned money to pay for the cigarettes. At the age of fourteen, I had a paper route and could smoke at home freely. This was a privilege that greatly impressed my friends. Two years later when they began to smoke, I was tired of it and, fortunately, decided to give it up.

In 1943, when I was seventeen, my mother died. My father remarried soon after and I enlisted in the Army. One month after reaching my eighteenth birthday, I volunteered for active duty.

On my Army "dog tags" was an "H" for "Hebrew," and that was about the extent of my Jewishness. I went to the synagogue the first week just to see who else was Jewish, but never returned after that. In that era, it was considered an accomplishment to be able to "pass" and seem not Jewish.

I was sent overseas in June, 1944, on "D-Day," but instead of landing on the beaches of Normandy, I landed in England as a replacement trainee. Shortly after that I was sent to France and served as a machine gunner in the 100th Infantry Division.

December 8, 1944 is a date I will never forget, it was on that day that our position was overrun and I was taken prisoner by the Germans in Alsace-Lorraine. Only three of us were captured. The rest of the unit either escaped or were killed.

Since I was a replacement, neither of my fellow captives knew my religion. The Nazi's special treatment of Jews was something I could do without, so the first thing I did when they began to march us along a road was throw away my dog tags.

Because I knew Yiddish, I understood a lot of what the enemy said, and could even speak the language to some extent. The main ancestor of Yiddish happens to be Middle High German, so many of the words are practically the same in both tongues. But a number of key Hebrew words have made their way into Yiddish too and I had to avoid letting any of these give me away. For instance, the German word for "perhaps" is vielleicht, as opposed to the Jewish efshar, and their word for "war" is krieg not milchamah.

In order to keep a low profile then, I listened a lot more than I spoke. The first words a German would say to me were Yud macht krieg, meaning "The Jews are making the war." Once, a German guard showed me a picture of Hitler and said, "Do you know who this is? He is the man who took everything from the Jews and gave it to us."

I really had to think fast in those days. The guards' way of being friendly or indulging in small talk was by making anti-Semitic remarks. When my fellow prisoners asked, "What did he say?" I'd quickly make something up, rather than translate those anti-Jewish statements. The Germans were so ingrained with anti-Semitism that they felt that anyone who opposed them must be a Jew. When President Roosevelt died in April, 1945, they came running into our barracks shouting, Rosenfeld ist tot. When I asked them who Rosenfeld was, they said President Rosenfeld. To them, he was a Jew named Rosenfeld.

When the Germans wondered where I had learned their language, naturally I couldn't reveal that I had picked it up from the Yiddish. Instead, I told them that I was a student.

One of them got suspicious. "If you are a student," he asked, "then why are you not an officer?" I looked down at the ground, as though I was ashamed to meet his eye. "Because," I said, "I drank too much." I must have convinced him, because he dropped the subject. Who knows? Maybe he had the same problem.

Funny what things came in handy. Two facts enabled me to barter: speaking German, French, and Russian (I studied the latter at college), and being a non-smoker.

Using a pair of wire-clippers, I would manage to crawl under the fence that closed off the other POW compounds. I would trade such items as cigarettes, rings, and watches for bread and potatoes. It was a risky act, but one I thought was well worth the danger to get the needed extra food for my fellow prisoners and myself.

Some of the other prisoners once asked me how much bread does a soldier get in the American Army and when I told him that the bread was on the table and that we could take as much as we wanted, you should have seen how amazed they were.

However, at that time, I also learned that crime does not pay. Believe it or not, while I was a POW, a group of us planned a burglary in the camp kitchen. I was asked to join them because I had a watch and the plan was to get as much food out in three minutes as we could because that is how long it took for the German guard to circle the area. We arranged with one of the cooks to close the kitchen window but not lock it and our group of six delegated two of us, one to climb in and one to stand outside, to get the goods. In three minutes we were able to get a tub of marmalade. We divided it equally-I received about one half of a quart. Because we were all afraid of getting caught, we planned to finish the marmalade that night so that if there was a search we would not be discovered. In the morning, when the Germans became aware of the theft, they punished all the prisoners by not giving them marmalade for their bread, despite the fact that only one out of ten jars was stolen. That night, because I ate so much marmalade, I developed tremendous diarrhea and never did get to enjoy the extra food. As I said before, crime did not pay. After we were liberated, we boasted that we were the perpetrators.

When people asked what lesson I learned from my POW experience I always say, "I'll never go hungry again," just like Scarlett O'Hara in the movie "Gone with the Wind." Ever since I was liberated, I have kept my word and only gone hungry on Yom Kippur (a Jewish fast day).

The next lesson I learned was cleanliness. In addition to the meager food rations allotted to us, we were never issued new clothes, so that I wore the same clothes for five months. Every week or so I would attempt to wash the clothes or boil them to get rid of the lice. Luckily, my clothes lasted five months since the army material was very strong.

Another thing I acquired as a POW was respect for the discipline necessary to keep dietary laws. Before I was captured, I was not "kosher" and did not keep the Jewish dietary laws. In the next barracks were British Indian prisoners who were taken at Dunkirk. They would not eat meat even under those deprived circumstances and it was my job to negotiate on behalf of the other prisoners to exchange our powdered milk cans (called "klim," which we occasionally got in the Red Cross parcels we received for the meat cans received by the Indians. We Americans, of course, preferred the meat while the Indians would rather have the milk. At that time I thought it was foolish of the Indians to give up the pleasures of meat. Now that I am "Kosher," I readily understand what principles mean to people regardless of the situation.

As an aside, the reason I was sent to the barracks next to the British Indians was because I spoke German. Believe it or not, the lower classes in India, even though they were part of the British Empire, did not speak English. However, after four years in captivity, they learned enough German for me to barter with them in German.[4]

---

[4] When the former head of the United Nations, Kurt Waldheim, stated that he was only an interpreter during the war and did not participate in any atrocities, it had to be untrue because you could get an

Another interesting thing was that as the Germans were advancing during the Battle of the Bulge, they would come into our barracks and state that this victory would be another winning situation like Dunkirk (a battle where all the British were driven out of France). We soldiers considered Dunkirk a victory for us because most of the British troops were able to escape. But to the German mind Dunkirk was their greatest victory because it resulted in the retreat of all Allied troops from the continent of Europe and the abandonment of all their equipment. Had the Battle of the Bulge resulted in another Dunkirk, the war would have lasted several more years.

While I was in the German army camp waiting to be transported back to the POW camp, I lived with Russian slave laborers who told me that Christmas would be coming soon.

I was shocked to hear that on Christmas Eve the Germans would take them to pubs, which they had done the year before. Recently, I learned that the Romans did the same thing to their slaves. Fortunately, I was transferred out of this camp before Christmas Eve. I did, however, meet some good Germans. After the war the Jews said, "Let's kill all the Germans." Someone then asked, "What about the good Germans?" The Jews replied, "For them we say Kaddish! (a prayer for the dead)."

Before I was captured, we were given a lecture on what to do if taken prisoner. We were told that the best time to escape was during the first week or so after being

---

interpreter for a slice of bread. That is why the joke is told: "Did you ever hear about the new disease that has been discovered - Waldheimers? You forget you were a Nazi."

captured, before getting to a permanent camp. Thus, after my capture, I climbed over a fence and headed for the woods with the intention of staying there until the Americans arrived at the place I was hiding. I waited one full day, but unfortunately, this was at the height of the Battle of the Bulge when the Germans were advancing and the Americans were retreating. I decided to walk in the direction of our lines, which was about thirty miles away. I met people who were laborers and I begged them for food. I was given one-half of a loaf of bread by a French POW who was working as a farmer. In those days, if anyone was working in the fields, we could assume it was not a German male since all Germans were in the army or overseers. The Frenchman advised me that the Germans were advancing and I decided to travel not only at night but also in the daytime to get to our lines sooner. As I walked, I saw dug-in positions (bunkers) which the Germans had prepared so that if they should fall back they were ready.

With the compass the French farmer gave me, I proceeded to walk night and day. When I was stopped by a policeman, I stated that I was a French POW working on a farm and had lost my way. When I was being questioned, one policeman said to the other that I did not speak German like a Frenchman. I was afraid that they might think that I spoke German like a Jew, and then I admitted to them that I was an American and that I had escaped from a temporary POW camp near Lundstahl. When I returned to camp, the sergeant asked me why I escaped. I did not realize that I was now safe because I was no longer in the battle, I was a prisoner. I responded that the reason I escaped was that I was crazy with hunger. He then asked me in German: Wie alt bist Du? ("How old are you?"). He used a familiar term du instead of sie (used when you address strangers). When

I told him that I was only 19 years old he said Ach, mein kind ("Oh, my child"), and instead of punishing me, he rewarded me with a loaf of bread. Of course, if he had known that I was a Jew, I would not have gotten such royal treatment.

After I had been a prisoner for about three months, an American soldier I hadn't seen around approached me.

"We're gonna be marched out of this here camp in a coupla days," he said. "I'm in charge of, you know, burials. So I hafta know what kind you'd want."

The question threw me. The thought of a cross over my grave hit me so hard that for the first time I admitted to someone there that I'm Jewish. By the way, this feeling I had gives me some insight into all the fuss about the 35-foot crucifix at Auschwitz, the death site for so many Jews.

Turns out this G.I. was working for the Germans. Next thing I knew, I was thrown into a cell with thirty-two other G.I.'s they thought were Jewish. Actually, only about twenty-five of us were. The others only looked like the Nazis' idea of a Jew. One happened to be an American Indian named Broadstone, and several others were Italian-Americans. The more they denied being Jewish, the more the Germans doubted their claims, even when they begged to be allowed to go to church.

At that time I learned about the Nazis' "ethnic cleansing" program. The British-Irish were separated from the British-English and from the South Africans. The Yugoslavs were divided into Serbs and Croatians.

The Croatians were sent home and no longer treated as POW's when the Germans declared Croatia a separate state and when Croatia joined the Axis. In addition, the Dutch and the Belgian-Flemish were considered Aryans and did not have to be put into POW camps; they were sent home to work on farms or in factories. The Alsatians in the French Army were also discharged, and subsequently the Germans drafted them into the German Army.

My three days' stay in the cell had one advantage-privacy. Sleeping in my own cell was much more comfortable than sleeping back-to-back on wooden boards with straw mattresses.

Our daily rations were I/6th of a loaf of bread and one bowl of soup. The other American POW's who had unsuccessfully protested our segregation found another way to help. The soup bucket was intended to hold 50 portions, but they filled it up to the brim. That way, the 33 of us each got an extra bowl.

In being marched out of the camp, we 33 were kept apart and to the rear. Until now, the knowledge that they were losing the war made the guards act more or less friendly to the prisoners from the victors-to-be. But now we began to see German cruelty for the first time.

We suspected Jews were the pariahs of the forced march. If any of us slowed down, he was beaten severely. Luckily for us, some of the other prisoners couldn't keep up the pace. As they fell back, they began to intermingle with us. Another thing that worked in our favor was the frequent changing of the guard. By the time we arrived at the new camp, the segregation was over.

This experience taught me two things-never to forget that I am a Jew, and to care about my fellow Jews. When I met my future wife, she thought I was a Gentile, until she saw me at a rally for the Warsaw Ghetto Jews.

Today people ask me if, at the time, I had ever heard of the Warsaw Ghetto uprising. In April 1943, I was a 17-year-old Jewish American boy and I was not informed of any Warsaw Ghetto revolution; it was never stressed in the American press or radio. As a matter of fact, we were told to discount most news about the killing of Jews as mere propaganda. Interestingly enough, I received the information about the Warsaw Ghetto from a Polish prisoner in the next barracks who mentioned his sympathy for the Jews who were killed there.

The Poles, when the Russians were about thirty miles from Warsaw, started their own revolution against the Germans with the hope that the Russians would advance quickly and free them. When little hope came and the Russians did not advance, they surrendered to the Germans with the understanding that the Polish revolutionaries would be treated as prisoners of war. I found out later that Britain dropped supplies by airplanes to Warsaw when these Poles were fighting the Germans, yet Britain did nothing to aid the Jews fighting in the Warsaw Ghetto. It is thus interesting to note that when Jews fought against the Nazi's they were massacred, but when the Polish revolutionaries fought against the Germans and then surrendered, they were treated honorably and became prisoners of war. The failure of the Russian Army to advance and try to help these Poles, although they were only 30 miles away, caused much hostility between Poles and Russians for many years after the war.

I remember back to 1946 when I was at Brooklyn College and saw a white, Jewish boy wearing a black armband. I asked him whether he was in mourning, and he told me "Yes, for the blacks who were lynched in the South." I then asked him what about the six million Jews who were murdered, and he told me, "That happened in Europe; that has nothing to do with us. The lynching happened in America and this concerns us."

Unfortunately, this was the attitude of many American Jews; they would demonstrate for civil rights and ignore Jewish suffering.

Since I was captured due to the negligence of the American Amy, I decided to become a negligence lawyer. I figured that I would have a lot of cases and be successful, since I had proof that even the best-meaning people can be negligent.

I didn't pay much attention to Lee at first. But when the second year came around, she had matured. When she came up to me and said, "Don't you remember me? I wrote you a poem...?" I took notice all right.

Although I had spent all of my life, except for my army days, in Brooklyn, I had never personally met anyone of the Orthodox persuasion. I admired and respected this very unusual young woman for her strong religious convictions.

She didn't comment on my lack of observance, and made no demands on me along those lines. At first. In fact, in a way, she was the best date I had ever had. I could take her in a treif (non-kosher) Chinese restaurant and get away with ordering dinner for one and two cups of tea.

At that time, the War for Israeli Independence was raging in what was then called Palestine. As an ardent Zionist, I thought I would join the Israeli Army and help fight the good fight. Lee, however, had other ideas, and talked me out of it.

The rest, as they say, is history.

CHAPTER 6
RELIGIOUS TRANSFORMATION OF HANDSOME HARRY

Harry says, "The rest is history." But, it should be noted, history didn't happen so fast.

Harry comes from a generation where to be an American meant shedding your roots and becoming part of the melting pot. People tried not to look too Jewish, and those who looked like what people imagined were Jewish types could not go far. From what I recall, everyone wanted a pug nose and blond hair. I think I represented all the qualities he disliked and didn't want in a wife. "I am your punishment," I always told him.

Very early in our relationship I had told Harry that I couldn't possibly bring him home to my parents as a potential son-in-law because my father was a rabbi and Harry wasn't Orthodox.

"Orthodox?" he asked, "What's that?" Actually, this is how I got him to date me, by promising him that I would never marry him. He was afraid that every girl had her eye on him for marriage, and he was not ready by far.

All the time that I was seeing the "dates" that my father kept providing, Harry was in the habit of secretly walking me home from school, or rather accompanying me to within a block of my house.

We kidded around a lot on those walks, but we spoke of serious matters too. For example, he persuaded me to switch my career plans and apply to his alma mater, Brooklyn Law School.

Little by little, I began to talk to my family about my great library find. Many years later, at our 25th anniversary party, my brother, Rabbi Benjamin Blech, publicly accused me of having stopped all education cold in our family.

"After my sister met Harry," he quipped, "none of us were permitted into libraries anymore."

Ultimately, my father arrived at two realizations. He knew that I was not likely to develop an enthusiasm for one of his shiduchim. He also understood that in becoming a law student, I had in effect narrowed my chances of appealing to one of those nice Orthodox boys, most of whom took a dim view of liberated women. And so my father finally consented to meet the man I loved.

With a doctor on-call in case of any heart attacks, Harry was ushered in before the assembled Blech family. My father's first words upon seeing Harry were: "oy iz er shain!"[5] (oh is he handsome). Upon seeing how truly good looking and nice Harry was, my father took him into his heart at once, naturally.

As he shook my father's hand, Harry said, "I will do whatever you teach me...mine is not to reason why; mine is but to do or die."

The unqualified willingness that he expressed in this promise is important. It echoes the vow the children of Israel were said to have made when G-d gave them the Torah.

Na'aseh ve nishmah, they said, "We will do and we will understand." Note the order of their twofold pledge: first

---

[5] Like father, like daughter!

comes performing the good deeds and keeping the commandments. Once that has become a regular way of life, then an understanding of why the Almighty wants us to observe these laws may follow.

It is interesting to note that one of the credos of Alcoholics Anonymous is based upon that precept in our Bible, since they teach their members to act as if. This means, act as if you are kind, etc., and it will automatically become part of your lifestyle.

At this point, Harry's basic training, amounting to a crash course in Orthodox Judaism with us as his guides, began. We issued him a kit consisting of a siddur (prayerbook), tallis (prayer shawl), and tefillen (phylacteries). He had to be watched, of course. For the next six months he just about lived at our house, and went home only to sleep.

Being an observant Jew is a fulltime, year-round commitment. The covenant our forefathers made with G-d in accepting the Torah is a bond that is everlasting-one that we renew with every prayer, with every performance of His commandments.

How do we know what these are? Besides the written Torah received on Mount Sinai, there is the oral Torah received on Mount Sinai and there is the oral Torah as it appears in the Talmud. But that is not all. There are also minhagim (customs) that impact observance in the home, in the synagogue, and in the outside world.

Though Harry's new chosen lifestyle was certainly a serious matter, it didn't have to be all solemn. For example, I thought of ways of penciling helpful comments in his siddur, in language he could grasp.

Thus, next to Kedusha, the holiest prayer, when we rise on our toes, I wrote in "ballet here." When we say the Amida, or silent standing prayer, we take three steps back to show our respect for the Almighty before whom we stand, and then three steps forward when we finish. Here, my notation was "cha, cha, cha."

By June of 1952, Harry First was deemed ready for marriage to the daughter of Rabbi Ben Zion Blech.

Incidentally, a challenge confronted my father the first Rosh Hashanah after our marriage. It was discovered that Harry was a Kohain (descendant of the priestly family) and as such, had special duties to perform at certain festivals. Together with the other Kohanim, he was expected to recite particular blessings before the entire congregation. These had to be done by heart and, of course, Harry did not know them.

For the Rabbi's son-in-law to be unable to fulfill his obligation would be quite an embarrassment. What was the solution? Under the huge prayer shawl of my father, as he stood before the congregation, were nothing less than 'TV-type cue cards prepared for Harry's eyes alone.

To his credit, he said the blessings so perfectly that no one guessed their secret. But after stepping down from the podium, he was heard to comment, "Well, that's show business..."

It is obvious that, even according to our tradition, Harry and I were well suited for each other. In years past, it had been the custom to test the prospective groom on his Bible learning and the prospective bride on her prowess as a cook. By those criteria, we were a perfect match. The fact was that he knew nothing of Bible study and I couldn't cook. Thus we began to plan for the ceremony that would mark the start of our life together.

CHAPTER 7
OUR WEDDING TAKES PLACE

Since I was a European girl who came from an Orthodox home, I had a dowry. But because of his background, Harry did not know enough to ask for it. Aside from his good looks, this silence was probably the only positive thing my father saw in Harry and is what helped him decide to give his consent. At our 25th wedding anniversary party, one of the verses of the song we performed went as follows:

> *"Lee had a dowry,*
> *Which they forgot to tell him too,*
> *And now it's too late For Harry to sue!"*

Incidentally, after we celebrated our 25th anniversary, my father finally told Harry that he would give him a dowry since he had proven to be a good husband.

"What would you really like?" he asked. Harry's answer pleased him no end. "I would love to have one of those silver collars for the prayer shawl that the very Orthodox men wear to shul." he said.

No sooner did my father put down the phone, than he ran to the local Judaica shop. He chose the most beautiful atara (tallis silver collar) that he was able to find.

On presenting it to him, my father innocently asked, "Now tell me Harry, what would you like for your fiftieth anniversary, if I live that long?"

With a straight face, Harry answered, "For that, I would like you to give me Smicha (a Rabbinic degree)."

"You, a rabbi? Not even in a hundred years!" thundered my father. One of the other versus sung by us at our anniversary illustrates the reason for this:

> *"Rabbi Blech tried to teach him*
> *Torah to learn*
> *But Harry was more interested in*
> *How much money he could earn."*

About four hundred people attended our wedding on June 24, 1952 at the Gold Manor in Williamsburg, Brooklyn. Harry was allowed one guest-either his father or his mother. Seriously, though, Harry did bring his entire family.

We arranged to meet Harry's father about a week before the wedding in order to explain that he was expected to pay for the music, the liquor, and the flowers. My family would foot the rest of the cost, a generous ten dollars per couple. That gentleman was not at all what we had expected.

The father of the great assimilated-American, Harry First, was a little old Jewish man with a Jewish newspaper folded under his arm. Although he had lived in this country some forty years, he still spoke only Yiddish.

Harry tells of the time they were in a subway station and his father asked a black conductor, Vie nemt men die train zu Times Skvare? Believe it or not, the conductor pointed them in the right direction.

Another surprising thing was Harry's father's name: Sam Goldberg. Really. The story is that he was born Sam First, but on arriving in America, he began working under his cousin's union book.

Before becoming a citizen, he was told that he could take any name he wanted. In many European countries, Jews were made to pay for their last names, which is why we have so many Goldbergs, Goldbaums, and Goldsteins (for Gold Mountain, Gold Tree, and Gold Stone). I guess my own ancestors were unable to pay very much because the name Blech (meaning "tin") has a cheaper connotation.

To my father-in-law, his cousin's name of "Goldberg" sounded much classier than his own "Firszt." Now, when people ask Harry how come his name is First while his father's name is Goldberg, he answers, "My father changed his name," and he isn't joking.

Speaking of names, it is said that after He created the world, G-d summoned Adam and asked him to name all the animals. Adam decided to name them according to what they did. He therefore named the donkey chamor, "a heavy burden," because that is what it carried. He called the horse suss, because the sum of that word's letters is the same as that of the letters in "to run fast," which is what horses can do.

When it came to naming himself, the first man chose Adam. Surprised, G-d asked, "If you named all the animals for their activities, why did you name yourself after "earth," which does nothing?"

Adam's beautiful answer was "It is true that earth all by itself is nothing, but you can let it be a desert or you can make it bloom. In the same way, a man can be nothing or he can be as great as he chooses to become."

Getting back to the wedding, creating the seating chart was a challenge, as is by most weddings. A comedian once said,

"We had to make thirty-eight tables-for-one." According to my brother, there's a good explanation for why our marriage has endured. It's because of the words Harry spoke under the canopy. Instead of harai at mekudeshet lee, meaning "Be thou consecrated unto me," he pronounced it, "HARRY at mekudeshes LEE."

After our wedding, we honeymooned in the Catskills at Grossinger's, where we had Shevah Bruches (special prayers said every evening during the first seven days after a wedding).

We began our life together in a small apartment on Ocean Parkway in Brooklyn. I continued Harry's Jewish education and every Saturday afternoon I would learn Pirke Avos ("The Sayings of the Fathers") with him. His favorite saying of one of the sages was, "Never talk too much to a woman.

Harry and I continued to study the Bible together. Since it was now the Jewish New Year, we read about the creation of the world. Right in the third chapter of Genesis, it says that Eve's punishment for tempting Adam with the forbidden fruit was twofold: "...in pain shalt thou bring forth children" and "thy desire shall be to thy husband, and he shall rule over thee."

Harry loved that second curse, but I went about looking for an explanation. The issue is: is a curse a command? In other words, must these two curses last forever as a G-d-given command, or is it foreseeable that women will ultimately free themselves from that yoke? Moreover, how do we reconcile the two curses with today's Women's Liberation Movement? Doesn't that sentence both date the Bible and diminish its appeal to women?

Here are some relevant comments that I came across. The question of the duration of "you will have pain in childbirth" arose when anesthesia was discovered in the last century. Was it permissible to use it in order to relieve the pain of childbirth? The Catholic Church said no, at first. The rabbis, on the other hand, said that since G-d gave us the knowledge to develop anesthesia, He would want it used for the benefit of mankind.

As for the second curse, the husband's ruling over the wife, is that to be forever? Before Eve's sin and subsequent punishment, she was equal in all ways to her husband. We believe that the ultimate goal of the world is the Coming of the Messiah, when we will revert to our living conditions in the Garden of Eden. Men and women were equal then and they had not been cursed.

Well, then, when we see women becoming increasingly liberated and acknowledged as equal partners in marriage and in the world at large, we should view that as a sign. Therefore, the more benefits women acquire through the Women's Lib Movement, the closer we get to the Coming of the Messiah!

One more Biblical thought relating to the subject of marriage. The word ish means "man" in Hebrew, and it is spelled with the letter yud in the middle. On the other hand, the word isha, which means "woman." is spelled with the letter hey at the end. Note that the letters yud and hey together are how the name of G-d is spelled.

Thus it follows that when a man and woman get together and recognize the need for G-d's presence in all their actions, their marriage will succeed. But, should we delete the two letters yud and hey from the words for man and woman we get the word aysh, which means "fire." Therefore, without morality, ethics, and the presence of G-d in their relationship, man and woman will consume each other as if by fire.

Such are the teachings that Harry and I would share as we studied the Bible together.

CHAPTER 8
I COMBINE MY CAREER WITH A FAMILY

In the previous chapter, we recounted the tradition of how Adam had named all the animals for their activities and then chose Adam (earth) for himself because, like earth, man can be nothing or he can be as great as he chooses to become.

Of course the term "man" here refers to the human race. Women, as well as men, possess nearly limitless horizons. In my case, I was studying to become a teacher of foreign languages when Handsome Harry persuaded me to apply to law school. This was a goal that had never entered my mind. Yet in 1954 I graduated from Brooklyn Law School with an excellent record (practically all A's).

I attended law school as a full time student and worked in Harry's office after classes. I cooked and cleaned and did all the housework. In those days, household duties were not shared by husbands and wives. No one would ever think of it. A home-cooked meal had to be on the table every night. Things are very different today.

The story is told about a man who is very sick and the doctor calls in his wife and children, but he speaks to the wife first, alone. The doctor says, "Your husband is gravely ill and he will die. However, if you do three things, his life can be spared: first, you must do whatever he says so he should not be aggravated. Second, you must greet him every single day, and third, he must get three home-cooked meals from you per day." The woman leaves the doctor and when she is greeted by her children they cry out, "Mother, what did the doctor say?" She coldly answers, "He said that Dad's gonna have to die."

Without taking a Bar Review course I managed to pass the Bar exam on my first try, whereupon Harry made me a partner in his law firm and changed its name to First and First. I still think that he should have hunted up other partners to enable him to name the firm First, Last, and Always.

After a while, Harry finally gave me time off to start a family. As our anniversary song indicates:

> *"Lee gave birth to three children*
> *On dates Harry chose,*
> *Time off was only permitted her*
> *When the courts did close."*

Luckily, in those days, the courts did close for summer vacations.[6]

When we were married six years, the happy event occurred and we were able to send out the first of our very funny Birth Announcements.

A NEW BABY
LEE AND HARRY FIRST
Announce the admission of a new
member into the firm of
FIRST & FIRST, ESQS.,
To wit: MITCHELL MARK
Admitted into the world court on
JULY 14, 1958
Sworn in at 6 lbs. 14 ounces, at the

---

[6] Today, the courts are open all year round.

>Flower Firth Avenue Hospital
>SPECIALIZING in the practice of
>pleading and loud crying-in
>preparation for trial work.
>HEARINGS may be heard daily at the
>residence of the Firsts.

As for my other two birth announcements, you can read them in the back of the book.

Since we were out of ideas for birth announcements, we had no more children. Besides, we had heard that every fourth child born in the world is messy and we thought it might be a bit hard for everyone to adjust.

Seriously though, I have always championed equal rights for women. If that makes me a feminist, then so be it.

I am reminded of the woman who confided that she had a strong desire to join the Women's Liberation Movement. "Then why don't you?" asked her friend. "Because my husband won't let me!" she wailed.

Bearing children did not interrupt my career. I went to court on a daily basis. In those days women were not that visible there. It was all too often that I had to explain to the presiding judges that I was the attorney and not the injured plaintiff. Because I looked very young, they used to address me as the "Infant."[7]

Once, when I was selecting a jury, my opposing counsel said to the jury: "Will the fact that my adversary is a beautiful young lady affect your verdict in any way?" One

---

[7] In those days, the age at which an infant was considered an adult was 21 years.

of the jurors candidly answered, "Maybe." In today's courtroom this could never happen, since no man is supposed to notice that his adversary is a female. All people are considered equal, and no distinction is made between the sexes. My poor husband, who is still not accustomed to all this, recently addressed a female lawyer as follows: "Young Lady, would you be kind enough to pick a jury with me at this time?" You should hear the tirade he received. "Don't ever call me a young lady again. I am a lawyer, just like you." I think that some of the women have gone too far.

This is true history. The first day my husband sent me to court as a lawyer on a case, when they called the case, I stepped up-one woman among 200 men. I answered the court calendar and the judge looked up and said: "I do not to speak to women lawyers, so please leave this courtroom at once and send your husband on this case." And I did leave the court and sent my husband. Little did he know, some years later I came back as a judge.

Even if there were some prejudices against me because I was a female, it did not phase me at all and I took it in stride-it was expected, and there was nobody we could turn to in order to rectify the situation. Things are so totally different today. I have observed that about one quarter of the attorneys in court are women, and these things are, of course, a change for the better.

I was active in many Bar Associations, and in 1976 I was elected President of the Bronx Women's Bar Association.[8] Many years ago there was a need for women's bar

---

[8] The title of this group has presently been changed to Metropolitan Women's Bar Association.

associations since they were not permitted to join the Men's Bar Associations. When I asked the Associations why, they flippantly told me that the Men's Bar Associations did not have a Ladies Room. Thus, the women formed their own Bar Associations, and when I became President, a male attorney who is very prominent and wanted the publicity, sued me to join the Women's Bar Association. He wrote me a very funny poem which The New York Times printed. Needless to say, we let him join us and now we have many male members.

As for my views on women's rights, they appear in the New York Law Journal of June 17, 1978, under the heading "Liberty Bell Rings for Women." It is a reprint of the following speech, which I made upon my installation as President of the Bronx Women's Bar Association.

"When George Bernard Shaw was once asked, 'What do you think of clubs for women?' he answered, 'Only if all other means of persuasion fail.'

We have come together again at our annual installation of the (Bronx) Women's Bar Association to tell all the male chauvinists of the world that they have "MSed" the boat. And as your president, I wanted, in this year of the Bicentennial, to summarize what I feel is the most significant achievement of this country's remarkable history.

As lawyers cherish the concept of liberty, it should certainly be noteworthy for us to recognize the principle immortalized on the Liberty Bell. 'Proclaim liberty throughout the land unto all the inhabitants thereof, comes from the Bible.

As a rabbi's daughter, who is deeply conscious of my Judaic heritage, I know that this ideal is rooted not only in awareness of the equal rights of all "personkind," but of the equal value and worth of both sexes, of men and women as well.

When the Biblical commentators analyze the text which describes Eve's being created from the rib of man, they discuss why it could have been from no other part of the body. If woman had been created from man's head, she would try to have dominion over him; if from his feet, man would assume that he could trample over her. Instead, she comes from man's side, so that they might recognize that the best relationship between the sexes is that of perfect equality, side by side, with neither seeking dominance or superiority.

After two hundred years of American existence, I am particularly pleased that we have at least caught up with this Biblical ideal. The bell rings tonight for liberty throughout the land onto women judges, women lawyers, and women leaders. Even though we know we are more gorgeous than men, we are willing to settle for simple equality. As professionals dedicated to the pursuit of truth, we feel that our field, in particular, has the most need of the fair sex because 'Beauty is truth, truth is beauty.' In Washington those who have but a small fraction of our skills earn $14,000 a year for their semi-professional services on oversight committees.[9] I pray that we will be

---

[9] At that time, it was discovered that some US Senators put females on their payrolls who could neither type nor do any other office work. There was a big investigation going on with regard to this fraud.

recognized not only for our beauty but for our brains as well.

It seems only right that the three birth announcements be juxtaposed in this chapter with the comments I made to my peers in a professional setting. After all, family and careers are the major items in the juggling act that so many of us modern American women find ourselves performing every day of our lives.

CHAPTER 9
HOW TO GET A MAID AND KEEP HER

During the twenty-five years that Handsome Harry and I were business partners, we were often asked how we liked that arrangement. My husband had a stock response: "Do you have a partner in your own business?" he would ask. "You do? ...So, tell me, at the end of the week, instead of splitting the money you took in, how would you like to be taking it all home? Enough said."

With our crowded work schedules and a family to bring up, household help was a necessity. It was also a commodity hard to come by until we hit upon a great plan. Since we both spoke several languages, we hired non-English-speaking help.

Our ad in the Jewish newspaper brought forth Rachel, a real Jewish mother. Now how would you like to have your mother or mother-in-law live with you and give you orders all the time?

"Your children are two and three years old already," she'd say. "A little candy chocolate can't hurt them." Or, "They don't need so many toys... You're only spoiling them."

The only problem was that she was not Orthodox and we had to teach her all our ways.

We couldn't ask her to turn a light on for us on the Sabbath because, being Jewish, she was as obligated as we were to keep the religious laws. One rule she grew to love was: no work on the Sabbath.

I heard of a lucky Polish Christian maid who so enjoyed having Saturdays off in this Jewish household that she decided to extend the glowing spirituality to her own day of rest. Now she works a five-day week.

Two more maid stories: the one-liner of a comedian, "I have a sleep-in maid, and all she does is sleep in." And the one about the maid with an exciting new job: "I'm working for Elizabeth Taylor," she told her friends. "Yeah? Who'd you serve? Who was at her house?" After she had reeled off an impressive list of celebrities, one of her listeners said, "Gee, I'd love to have been there. What subjects did they kick around?" "It's a funny thing," she said, "but all they really talked about was us." "What do you mean, us?" "You know, the problem of getting and holding onto good household help!"

After Rachel, our next maid was Spanish-speaking Maria from Colombia. I had learned that language in school and now invested in a Spanish/English dictionary, which I grabbed whenever I had to give her instructions.

Maria's linguistic limitations proved to be both good news and bad news. On the positive side, we had all the conversational privacy that anyone could want. On the other hand, she was completely unable to answer the phone for us. That is, B.B. (Before the Brainstorm). What we did was assign each friend and relative a Spanish number. Then, she could tell us, "Numero cinco called" and we would know who it was.

When the kids got older, we had another bright idea. We paid them a nickel for each message they took. You should have seen how they fought over whose turn it was. We had to pay up, too.

We decided on this idea because of all the times we've called friends and left word with a child, only to learn later that the message was never delivered. The plan may work well for other parents, too, except that nowadays, a nickel would never do-you would have to up the ante quite a bit.[10]

In some ways things got easier as the kids grew older. When they were young, every maid's day off brought anxiety. I'd be worrying whether she'd be coming back the next day and on time. I truly had to be in court every day. As far as I was concerned, when she was late, she might just as well not have arrived at all-my day was shot.

The only way around this problem was to instruct each maid to come home the same night from her day off, no matter how late the hour. Thus, if she didn't arrive by the next morning, I had to pack our three kids in diapers and head for Boro Park. Here, my father, who was always home learning Torah, would take over for me until 5 PM. Then, after being in court all day and running my law practice, I'd dash over to Brooklyn. Naturally, I would then have to prepare and serve dinner, bathe the kids, and put them to bed. A challenging day.

---

[10] This reminds me of a depression story. In those hard times, a lady in a grocery reached into a barrel and asked, "How much for this pickle?" "A nickel," replied the grocer. Thinking she'd do better, she found a smaller one, and asked, "And how much for this pickele?" To which he answered, "A nickele."

CHAPTER 10
PARENTING WITH PLEASURE

When the children all reached school age, we found it difficult to get live-in help. We solved that problem by placing an ad in the local paper saying, "Household help wanted from 4 P.M. to 8 P.M. every day."

An amazing number of people responded, from sixteen-year-olds looking for after-school work to women in their sixties eager to earn a few dollars on the side.

After making my choice, here is how I organized her schedule. She would arrive at 4 P.M. and prepare our meal which we would eat at 5 P.M". Then she'd spend the next three hours cleaning the house. This plan worked out very well, because a) it wasn't too costly, and b) we all got our work done. We had to hire babysitters additionally, though.

After a number of years, we could let the kids be their own babysitters when we went out for a couple of hours in the neighborhood. We paid them each twenty-five cents an hour to ensure smooth going.

Upon our return we'd ask, "Were there any fights?" The answer was always, "No," because they wanted their money.

To manage as a working mother, one has to be flexible and avoid automatically adopting the so-called normal way of doing things. When each child was born, my husband and partner gave me only one week off. As a matter of fact he even brought work for me to the hospital! At this point, I found myself driven by two strong desires: I strongly wanted to keep up with my profession and I dearly wanted to spend as much time with my children as I possibly could.

Was this do-able? We found a way. Instead of our babies being put to bed at 6 P.M., we had them take two naps each day, one in the morning and one in the afternoon. When we came home at 5 o'clock, they were wide awake. I gave them baths, fed them and didn't put them to sleep until 10 P.M.

Because I had been out all day, housework and mothering were not drudgery to me. Being home was a novelty and a joy. But on Fridays, the one day I stayed home from work all day, Harry would come home to a frazzled wife. I think that being home full-time makes one tired.

Somewhere I read that we get energy by expending energy and I fully believe it. The more we do, the more we find ourselves able to do. To me, the rhythm of six days of purposeful activity, followed by one day of meaningful rest equals a good life.

We always made a practice of spending the Sabbath with our children. In fact, when Mitchell was born the first words out of his father's mouth were, "When can I take him to shul?"

Every Saturday, just about half an hour before the end of services (to minimize the risk of disturbing others), our maid would bring our kids to the synagogue. Harry and I could enjoy their company and teach them our ways at the same time.

We all need a day off for spiritual renewal. It's a way of emulating the Creator Who rested on the seventh day. The Christians consider Sunday their Sabbath; for the Moslems, it's Friday. I understand that in post-Revolutionary France, during the Reign of Terror, they tried to institute a different schedule based upon a ten-day work week. It failed, of course, because it violated the G-d given pattern.

By the way, the Bible contains a seeming contradiction. First, it tells us that G-d rested on the seventh day, and then it says that He completed the world on the seventh day. How can that be? Wasn't the world completed in six days?

The explanation is that by the end of the sixth day, the physical aspect of the world was created. On the seventh day, G-d added spirituality. Thus, it is a fallacy to laze around in bed all day Saturday under the impression that we have observed the commandment to keep the Sabbath. We must enrich our minds on that day, a process that separates us from the animal kingdom.

According to a rabbi whose lecture I attended, we are failing to allow ourselves the leisure of thought. We come home from work and what do we do? We immediately turn on the radio. Then, we'll read the newspaper. Next, we'll go out jogging, making sure to put on a headset first so that any possible thoughts may be driven out by music. He even saw one person jogging, listening to music, and reading a book at the same time.

If you came into a room, saw someone just sitting quietly and asked what he or she was doing, how would you react if the answer was, "I'm thinking..."? Would that answer seem strange? There is no reason at all why it should.

Actually, we benefit on many levels-mentally, emotionally, and physically-by stepping away regularly from the busy workday "rat race" in order to take stock of ourselves. It's good to ask ourselves once a week: "What is my purpose here? Where am I going?"

Our involvement in spiritual matters on the Sabbath doesn't have to consist only of learning or heavy discussion. Today, there are games on the market, e.g., Jewish Trivial Pursuits, that make for family fun.

I was once teaching Bible to an interested friend and, after an hour, I asked her whether she thought she would remember any of it. By way of answer, she likened studying to filling a bottle with water.

"When you empty the bottle, the inside is still wet. A few drops of the liquid always remain," she said.

I liked her analogy. It makes sense to be teaching our children more and more of our values-we keep hoping for the best. Our prayer is that no matter what emptying influences they encounter later on in life, what they've learned at home will remain with them.

Sometimes a single letter of the Hebrew alphabet can carry a meaningful message. Take lamed ("|"), the final letter in the last of the Five Books of Moses. Lamed is also a word that has two meanings: "to learn" and "to teach." The message? After we have finished learning the Bible, we have the obligation to teach it.

It's interesting, too, that the numerical value of the word lamed is the same as that of the word ade, Hebrew for "to bear witness." Thus, we must not only teach good deeds, but must also bear witness by our actions that we have learned them ourselves.

In parenting, this means doing our best to avoid the "do as I say, not as I do" syndrome. Harry and I therefore tried to set a good example for the kids-not that they were always quick to follow our lead. Though they saw us say the blessings over food all the time, and saw us regularly say our prayers, they always managed to do likewise.

Whatever methods I employed, I really did make an all-out effort for them to be perfect. As one of my friends quips, "It looks like they took it seriously, while you were only kidding."

Our children really did turn out very well. All three lead wholesome Torah-true lives and are doing a great job of raising their own kids.

That's why while our parents look at their grown children and wail, "Where did I go wrong?" Harry considers ours and wonders, "Where did I go right?"

As it happens, I have an answer. He should have known what to expect when he married me. It is said that when you marry the daughter of a Talmud chachum (wise religious man), your children will take after their maternal grandfather.

The saying refers to the hereditary aspect of life. True, the genetic make-up of a seedling is important, but in order to reach its full potential it needs to have a nourishing environment as well. Because we believed that the same truth applies to child rearing, we pitched in to help, found a nursery school, a kindergarten and then a Day School (yeshivah) at the Riverdale Jewish Center [with the aid of its rabbi, Dr. Jack Sable].

The next stage of our children's education presented a problem. We had so many students that we were bursting at the seams and could no longer fit into the synagogue rooms. Thus we needed a larger school building. As we saw it, we had two options: move or get busy building a new school in our beloved Riverdale.

We chose the latter path, and with the help of some very generous people managed to acquire the Toscanini estate. Here, the Salanter Akiba of Riverdale (S.A.R.) was built, and the word for the school was "gorgeous!"

The building itself is light on interior walls between classrooms in order to reflect an open, less structured approach to education. Instead of being locked into particular classes by age, each child progresses at his or her own pace. Anyone who shows special strength or interest in a subject area beyond what his age group has reached, moves right along to the next level.

This approach is totally in keeping with the Jewish teaching that each child be brought up according to his derech (way). One should not expect all four-year olds to be able to read just because some can do so. Nor should the father of an older son say, "Well, since I never had the chance or inclination to study medicine, it's better that my son not become a doctor either."

According to the rabbi whom I heard explain it, "Each person must do what he desires according to his needs, as long as his derech lies within the precepts of our morality."

Another educational policy at S.A.R. is the absence of grade-giving. The school works on the "contract" plan where teachers and individual students draw up and agree to a series of goals to be reached.

Since there were no formal report cards, the only way I could find out how my kids were doing was via the periodic parent-teacher conferences. Naturally, our children took great interest in these events. Whenever I returned from one, I would be sure to find them waiting for me.

"So, what did the teacher say about me this time?" they would ask.

Time for another brainstorm. Being an attorney enroute from work, I invariably arrived at the conference carrying a briefcase. Unbeknown to anyone, I quietly tucked in a recorder and taped all the sessions. Now all of the children could (and did) listen in on the discussions over and over again to their hearts' content. Excellent as S.A.R. is, nothing about it prepared our kids for the shock of high school. Upon entering Ramaz, a Manhattan day school, they went from a no-grade learning environment to a keenly competitive one. Where did they fare better? Results were mixed. Mitchell and Shari did extremely well in both settings. However, I think at S.A.R. that the teachers got to know the students better individually.

As for Seth, he was somewhere in the middle all along. On entering Yeshiva University, though, he became a genius. All of his grades were excellent. I think the explanation is that he was now a highly motivated student, I am convinced that this factor can make all the difference in the world.

What happened was that Seth spent his senior year at a Yeshiva in Israel where he studied the Bible, Jewish Law, and Jewish History. He discovered that he loved it all-even more than baseball. As a result, he abandoned his earlier plan to attend an Ivy League college and registered at Y.U.

There was only one problem, in my opinion. He fell in love with Israel and, after his marriage, decided to make aliyah (emigrate to Israel).

It's hard for some of us parents to accept the fact that we cannot possibly live our children's lives for them. If we could, that would probably be bad for all concerned. Once we've learned that lesson, we're in business. We can then go back and build our own lives. Having married off all three of our children, Harry and I are just about beginning to accept that challenge.

CHAPTER 11
SETH AND SHARI FIND MATES

It's no secret that when I first brought Handsome Harry home, he was not exactly what my father would have chosen for me. My husband has known this fact all along. In fact, when we were honored at a U.J.A. dinner after being married some twenty-five years, someone brought the subject up.

"Tell me something, Harry," he asked," does your father-in-law accept you yet?"

"I think so." He answered. "He is beginning to introduce me as his son-in-law."

Somehow, it seems harder for European than for American parents to accept their children's doings. In our case-well, let's begin with our youngest, who was the first to get married.

When Seth was 21 he went off on a weekend with some other young people who were interested in moving to Israel. At the dinner table, he asked someone to please pass the salt. When she did, he found himself looking into the gorgeous eyes of a young woman. Losing no time, he invited her to go for a walk with him. I never asked whether they had finished their meal first.

On his return home two days later, our son announced that he had found the girl of his dreams, a girl very much like his mother. ("Then I'll probably like her and his father will probably hate her," I thought.)

"What special qualities about her do you admire?" we asked.

That is when Seth described Eta as being "beautiful, smart, a good person, and able to speak Yiddish."

They were married shortly after that meeting. That was eight years ago, and they are still very happy.

Seth, by the way, is a writer, editor, Bible student, computer expert and teacher. All in all, he has always been a source of joy for us.

Next, there's our daughter, and that's another chapter, or more likely another volume. Shari (Sarah) was a perfect daughter, and became a Lubavitcher (Chassidic and a disciple of Rabbi Schneerson).

She began taking courses in the Crown Heights section of Brooklyn. One day, she phoned us from there to say that she had good news. What was the news? She was engaged! It seems that her teacher had introduced her to a young man, and they hit it off. So, as is the Chabad custom, they wrote their names on a slip of paper to be handed to the Rebbe and waited.

In this case, his opinion was that this was a favorable match. That's all they needed. Needless to say, we were a little surprised when Shari and Yossi went ahead and began making wedding plans. Then she told us that she was especially happy about his lineage, namely that he's a relative of Rabbi Schneerson and a descendent of the original father of the Chabad movement.

When we saw that she was serious about the marriage and heard what a fine family he comes from, we relented.

First off, we were surprised by a phone call from Rabbi Schneerson's emissary, telling us that we could have a private audience with the Rebbe. We had no idea what a great honor this is until we began telling our friends about it.

Then we learned that people travel from all across the world to see the Rebbe and receive his blessing. They wait months and months for the chance to be in his presence.

The day came, and our entire family went for the audience. As might be expected, we were filled with curiosity. Imagine our surprise when we got there and the Rebbe grabbed my husband and took him to the front of the synagogue to pray beside him.

Upon beholding this sight, my father was nothing short of amazed.

"If Harry First is praying with Rabbi Schneerson, the world famous Lubavitcher Rebbe," he shouted, "then there is no question about it. The Messiah is definitely coming!"

CHAPTER 12
SHARI'S WEDDING-LUBAVITCH STYLE

My daughter's wedding was like something out of Fiddler on the Roof, with us as the players. The ceremony had to be in front of the Rebbe's study in Crown Heights-in the street. A platform with movie lights was set up on this sidewalk on Eastern Parkway. Any passerby was free to join the event.

This being a rather poor section of Brooklyn, I remarked to a couple of young Lubavitchers standing beside me that we had sunk to a new low. Our son's Bar-Mitzvah had taken place on the Star Lite Roof of the Waldorf Astoria Hotel. "No." said one of them. "This time you have reached even greater heights!" It all depends on your point of view.

Though he knew that the wedding would be taking place in the street, Harry insisted on wearing a tuxedo when walking his daughter to the chupa (canopy).

Our Riverdale friends "followed suit," with the result that we had two groups of guests, one in Chassidic garb and one in formal wear. No need to ask, "Which side are you from?" at this wedding.

I had invited everyone, along with friends and family-every co-worker, every lawyer who appeared before me. With all of the "drop-ins" free to stop by, it was a well-attended affair.

As for the wedding dinner, it was held a few blocks away at the Brooklyn Jewish Center. We had invited five hundred people and since the Lubavitchers do not make a practice of sending response cards, we just booked the entire place with open seating.

One of the Lubavitcher customs stems from the conviction that no party can be a truly happy occasion without some poor people being able to enjoy it too. The way it works is that two long tables are set up, one for fifty men and the other for fifty women. Anyone of the community who happens to be in need just sits down and partakes of the meal. In this manner hungry area residents can probably attend wedding or bar-mitzvah festivities several nights a week.

In this connection, a funny thing happened to us in Israel a few years later. We were introduced to a wealthy young Californian who gave us a warm hello. "I was at your daughter's wedding," he announced. "Really? Were you a friend or a relative of Yossi's?" we asked. "Neither," he said with a smile. "I went as one of the poor people."

This bride and groom certainly made a handsome couple. Of course, not everyone has the fortune to be born with good looks. As one well known comedian says, "Here I am, ugly as can be. Yet I have three beautiful children. Boy am I lucky my wife is gorgeous!"

Shari and Yossi have been married ten years and live in Israel. When their first child was born, I was delighted to be introduced to a gorgeous blond granddaughter.

They went on having beautiful babies and now have four daughters and one son. The latter is every bit as good looking as my husband.

But he'll grow up to look like a Lubavitcher, with a beard and side-curls," I wailed to my brother. "Won't it be funny to have a Lubavitcher in this world who resembles Handsome Harry First?"

Leave it to my brother to come up with a memorable comment. "G-d has a strange sense of humor," he said.

CHAPTER 13
MITCHELL FINDS A BRIDE

Our firstborn son was the last to get married. Speaking objectively, I have to say that he is the most wonderful human being in the world.

There are a few people who happen to be just plain good from the day that they are born-Mitchell is one of them. He never heard of sibling rivalry. When his sister and brother were born, he took them under his wing. He showed them so much love and care that one of the teachers at S.A.R. was compelled to call me. "I've never seen anything like it," she said. "No one else I know has a brother as good as your son Mitchell." After S.A.R. and Ramaz, Mitchell went to Columbia University and then to Columbia Law school. He always got excellent grades. Then came two years of study at a yeshiva in Israel where he took the first part of the Israeli Bar.

In many ways, Israel is like one big family.

Get on a bus and you'll find strangers talking to you. Some of these conversations can get pretty personal.

Thus it was that Mitchell found himself describing to the young woman sitting next to him just the kind of life partner he was looking for.

"She has to be an Orthodox Preppy," he said, "and I don't think that there are too many of them here in Israel."

"You're right," she said. "As it happens, I know the perfect bride for you, but she's in New York."

What are the odds that this encounter would lead to anything? But Mitch took down the phone number, made the call on his next visit home, and voila!-one match made.

This daughter-in-law, Sharon, is fabulous. She does not speak Yiddish, however, being a third or fourth generation American from Ohio.

It's interesting that although they were well educated, her parents were not Orthodox. As a result of the miraculous victory of the Six Day War, however, they did some rethinking, and gradually have become very observant.

In tracing their ancestry, they discovered that her mother is a descendant of Yeshiah Horowitz, the Shla, Chief Rabbi of Jerusalem in the 1620's. Today, the whole family is part of the growing number of "B.T's" (baalei tshuva, or returnees to the faith, as distinguished from the "F.F.B's," or frum from birth, among the Orthodox).

After his marriage, Mitchell left the firm that he had been working for and became a partner in First & First. Poor Handsome Harry. Before, he had to split the profits with his wife, and now he had to split them with his son.

Mitchell and Sharon live in Teaneck, N.J. with their sons Shaya and Daniel and daughter Rachel Tiferet.[11] These are our only American grandchildren.

Our other grandchildren are sabras (native born Israelis). We don't get to see them as often as we'd like, but we do

---

[11] When I mentioned to my brother how unusual I thought the name Tiferet, he answered "that's as close to 'gorgeous' as they could come--it's nice to have a grandchild named after me." In Hebrew tiferet actually means "splendor," but my brother took some poetic license at my expense.

make a point of visiting Seth, Shari and their families a couple of times a year.

In making aliyah, my son, daughter and their prospective spouses were spurred by idealism. It was not easy for them to say goodbye to the friends and family they had here. I'm sure they did not expect life to become so financially burdensome and had truly thought to be able to make it on their own.

The fact is, however, that Handsome Harry bought them each a new home, and is continuing to subsidize both families. My husband, who has worked hard all his life, had no complaints except for one instance. He expressed some doubts when Seth quit his job in order to study the Bible full time.

Seth's wife handled the friction in her own way, namely by explaining what will happen in the hereafter "When we die and go to heaven," said Eta, "our past lives are evaluated. We are deemed to be on a certain level, and given our reward. At this point, we can no longer enlarge our reward by doing good deeds. But suddenly, as we're seated there in heaven, a packet of jewels will be delivered to us. This is the reward we merit because our surviving children are still doing good deeds and studying the Bible."

I find the thought beautiful enough to soften the fact that we still have to help support our children.

There is a joke going around Israel today about the full-time Bible students (called Kollel Boys) whose wives must work to support them. The saying is that the Kollel Boys are trying to bring back polygamy. Do you know why? Because they can't live on the salary of just one wife.

There is a quip about grandparenting that usually gets a laugh: "Why is it so hard to become a grandparent?" "Because you have to rely on your children to do it for you."

In our case though, we don't laugh. We really can rely on our children to fulfill the biblical commandment, "Be fruitful and multiply."

Incidentally, why does it tell us to be fruitful and to multiply? Don't they mean the same thing?

The answer is that there is no redundancy here; the two commandments have different meanings. "Be fruitful" means have children. "Multiply" means duplicate yourself in your children. In other words, teach them your own good ways so that like you, they may know them.

This is what our own children are doing. I know I'm paying them the supreme compliment when I say that I hope they'll be as successful with their children as we have been with ours.

CHAPTER 14
CELEBRATING MY ANNIVERSARIES

I love people and make friends easily. One of my big regrets in life is that everyone's busy schedule makes it hard for us to get together before chunks of time go by. My solution? I give parties-big ones. To honor our still being happy residents of the state of matrimony, we have had three really big celebrations.

The first one was on June 26th, 1977, celebrating 25 years of marriage. To honor the occasion my husband commented, "Here I am married 25 years and it seems like yesterday-and you all know what a lousy day yesterday was!"

At that time I was an Administrative Law Judge at the New York State Workers' Compensation Board. As always, our invitations were an important detail since they set the theme of the event. Once the theme was decided, the rest of the plans just about fell into place. Knowing that those little come-ons which arrive in the mail set the tone, I'll admit I spend a lot of time, effort and imagination on them.

Since my husband is a practicing negligence attorney and I am a judge, we decided to spoof our professions. When I became a judge, all the mail was addressed as "Hon. Lee and Mr. Harry First," according my husband no title at all. Since my husband is a very good-looking guy, one of my friends hit upon the idea of calling him "Han. Harry First," for Handsome Harry First. From then on, all our friends followed suit and tons of mail comes to us addressed in this manner.

We booked our local synagogue and arranged for a real wedding, complete with wedding canopy, a sit down dinner and dancing. When anyone asked my husband why he wanted to have another wedding he said, "Everyone else has been married a few times!"

It is the custom among Jews that under the wedding canopy, at the conclusion of the service, the bridegroom breaks a glass for good luck. It was said at our celebration that Harry First was the only bridegroom in the history of the world who cut his foot on the glass and made a case out of it!

For this party our invitation took the form of a summons, the cause of action being to renew the marriage contract. We also played up the name "First." We always give out a souvenir at our parties, just some little trinket, since everyone loves to hold onto something to remember the affair. For this event we ordered ball point pens inscribed "the first twenty-five years are the hardest" (double entendre, of course). Since for a 25th Anniversary you are not setting up housekeeping, there was no necessity for us to receive any gifts. We stated on the invitation that "Your presence is our present."

I wore a pure white gown (if you're gonna do it, you do it right: I borrowed a headpiece and veil as well). The funny thing is that when my girlfriends got the invitation they also wanted to get into the act and have fun. They begged me to act as bridesmaids. This got my husband a little nervous and he shouted, "But I'm not paying for their gowns!" And so, they marched down in unmatched gowns, which even added to the fun.

I also had a maid of honor, my daughter. As for the ceremony itself, my parents walked me down the aisle. Harry, on the other hand, was brought down in handcuffs by my two sons. You should have heard the laughter in the audience. I then prevailed upon Judges and Rabbis to say a few words and the humor that emanated from each one was hilarious.

One rabbi stated, in a serious tone, "Many of you have been wondering why this couple is being married for a second time. They, on the other hand, are probably wondering why they got married the FIRST time.

Another judge announced, "I believe in marriage because a wife is only for the duration of a marriage, but an ex-wife is forever."

Then Harry, the happy bridegroom, quipped, "I think every man should get married 'cause otherwise a man might go through life thinking he had no faults at all!"

I then added, "Love may be blind, but marriage sure is an eye opener.

Harry and I then rendered an appropriate song as

follows (to the tune of "Down in the Valley"):

THE FIRST 25 YEARS ARE THE HARDEST

This is the story of how Harry and Lee met.
She went to the Brooklyn College Library,
But books she didn't get.
She took out the Best Seller
A real handsome fella
Whose name was Harry,
Whom at once she wanted to marry.

It took three years for her father to approve.
To learn to be "kosher"
Into Lee's house he had to move.

Rabbi Blech tried to teach him
the Bible to learn,
But Harry was more interested in how much
money he could earn.

Down at the Gold Manor, a catering hall in
Williamsburg,
Ten dollars a couple,
Was all Lee's parents would splurge.

Lee had a dowry,
which they forgot to tell him too,
And now it's too late, For Harry to sue.

Lee gave birth to three children,
On dates Harry chose,
Time off was only permitted her,
When the courts did close.

They practiced law together,
and made a lot of dough,
So the good things in life
Lee could always show.

Twenty-five years ago,
Lee and Harry began to play.
Let's hope they continue
Another 25 years this way.

Our 25th Anniversary Wedding was such a success that the entire community did not want the fun to end. They threw us a Post Nuptial Party where they made speeches praying for our continued fertility which, thank G-d, did not come to fruition.

We continued to throw parties on different themes for five years, and then came our 30th Wedding Anniversary. Our friends insisted, "make another wedding," and we, of course, obliged.

What theme could I think of? I finally came up with, "Come celebrate the End of the Thirty Year War-Peace At Last." My two Maids of Honor carried a sign: "Make Peace Not War. "The date was June 19th, 1982.

No matter the date of my anniversary, I always try to pick a weekend date for the party. This was also a catered affair in our synagogue with music and dancing. My husband, this time, was a captured prisoner. He was brought down the aisle by my two sons who held a gun to his head while the band played "I Surrender Dear." My parents again accompanied me down the aisle. In a pure white gown I carried a large sign stating "I Came, I Saw, I Conquered." The band played the "Battle Hymn of the Republic," glory, glory, hallelujah. As for our souvenir, we made up a keychain for each guest in the form of a heart imprinted "Every man must have his 'Peace'."

One of the other rabbis said, "When I first met Lee she told me she had made the acquaintance of Handsome Harry and asked innocently, 'How can I find out what he really thinks of me?' So I told her, "Marry him and you'll find out soon enough." I only picked those rabbis and judges who had a sense of humor, as you can see.

Harry then stood up and with all sincerity announced, "Man is not complete until he's married-and then he's finished."

Another rabbi said, "Their 30 years of marriage seems like only one day: Yom Kippur (a solemn and sad fast day on the Jewish calendar).

My late, beloved father had his own brand of wit: "Did it have to take 30 years, as in this case, to see if this marriage would work out? I have heard of the Six Day War, or other wars that lasted a few days. But who needed a Thirty Year War?" My father then added, "I have always hoped and prayed to bring my daughter to her wedding, but with three children accompanying her?"

My father then continued to explain: "According to the Bible, G-d is the bridegroom and the Torah is the bride. We received the Torah from Mt. Sinai on Pentecost, which is in the spring, and yet we do not celebrate our receiving of the Torah until the fall, on the holy day of Simchat Torah. Why do we have to wait so long? The answer is that in a union between two people there is a waiting period to see if, in fact, the marriage will work out. One cannot adjust to another or to the status of marriage immediately. Thus we give it a chance and wait for about six months to make sure that the Jewish nation is happy and wants to fully accept all the laws of the Torah. However, in the case of my daughter, did it have to take her 30 years to adjust?"

One of my brothers then stepped forth and spoke: "Lee's parents objected to the marriage because Harry was not too religious. Lee's father said that Harry did not even know the difference between heaven and hell, to which my mother answered, 'Let him marry Lee and she'll teach him what hell is!'"

When the Rabbi of the Riverdale Jewish Center spoke he stated: "This is definitely a FIRST for me. I wish to point out that this is the third time that Lee is marrying Harry and, under Jewish Law, if something is done three times, it is a Chazakah, which means it definitely becomes permanent."

One of the rabbis, viewing so many rabbis present, stated, "I haven't seen so many rabbis assembled at the Riverdale Jewish Center since there was an opening for a spiritual leader at that synagogue."

He went on, "Lee and Harry have been a continued source of inspiration to all law students. Because THEY could pass the Bar, that means anyone can."

When we were married 40 years, things were a little too quiet for me, so I decided to drum up some fun. I asked my husband if he could think of a 40th Anniversary party, and he suggested, "Forty years have I been in the desert, but I have not seen the Promised Land." Of course. The invitation read.

> **LET'S TOAST 40 YEARS**
> 40 years Harry has been in the desert, but he has not yet seen the Promised Land. To continue this odyssey, come and celebrate the remarriage of Lee and Harry First, to be held in the desert of Club El Morocco. We have had 40 years of wedded bliss. So this is one party you don't dare miss. To continue the usual trend, we have invited each and every gorgeous friend.

As you can see, since Harry was still in the desert, I picked the event space named "El Morocco" to signify the desert. When I walked down the aisle, I held up a big sign: "I Never Promised Him a Rose Garden." The wedding was performed by my brother who alighted on the stage and said, "People, you must be quiet now-remember you are not in synagogue. Lee is taking her time coming down the aisle; she must be thinking it over after 40 years."

I did have bridesmaids, and to top it off one of my dearest friends, Judge Maria McCarren, was my flower girl. My Maids of Honor were my sister-in-law and my dear friend, Madeline Title.

My brother continued: "We've tried and shall continue to try to marry them off until they get it right.

There is a word, which according to Lee, defines our world. Do you know that in fact it also defines our faith? The word is 'gorgeous.' If we write this word with Hebrew letters and add up the numerical value of each letter the total is 613- the total number of mitzvahs (good deeds) in the Torah which a Jew is obligated to keep. And this symbolizes the conduct of my sister Lee.

Harry and Lee have three gorgeous children. Mitchell is a tzadik. Do you know when he became a lawyer he took Lee's place and started to work for Harry, and we all know what a difficult task that is. As in A Tale of Two Cities by Charles Dickens, Sidney Carton gave his life for a great ideal. So Mitchell also said 'take me, take me,' and thereby freed Lee from slavery. It was a major breakthrough. However, her other two children went to live in Israel and although they could not emulate Mitchell they also say 'take, take, take.'

The secret of their life is that they have lived like in the movies:
'Europa, Europa' (Lee was born there)
'A Streetcar Named Desire' (Lee saw Harry)
'Crazy For Him'
'Conversations With My Father' (when my father found out about Harry)
'War and Peace' (until permission for the marriage was granted)
'Casablanca' (when she asked her father where to live and he said, 'far away')   'Cover Up'
'My Cousin Vinnie' (we didn't introduce Harry as a member of our family so fast)
'Rocky I, Rocky II, Rocky III' (to describe their marriage)
'Class Act' (this is the perfect description of their life)

My sister wants to make people happy and that is why she has made this party. She is willing to do this to entertain all her friends. The Torah comes in five books, Chamisha Chumshe Torah. What is Chamisha? It is five, and when we take those letters it makes the word simchah. That person who brings joy to the world has kept the whole Torah! This is my sister."

There were lots of laughs at these affairs and that's good. I see so much trouble around, both in and out of court, that I really like to go out of my way to lighten things up. There isn't a person I know, including Harry and myself, who has not experienced some sort of heartbreak. That's why I think we should all make the most of good times and why I'll never miss an occasion to celebrate. To reach such a milestone and to be married for 25 years and 30 years and 40 years to the same man is definitely such an occasion.

CHAPTER 15
LET'S GO TO MY PARTIES

In order not to lose contact with my friends, I have two annual get-togethers with them every year and entertain 70 of them at each of the parties. Luckily, Handsome Harry loves these bashes too and sometimes it's hard to tell who's having more fun, the guests or the hosts. Hospitality, by the way, has long been a Jewish virtue, one that we associate with Abraham, Father of the Jewish people. Maybe that's another reason why Harry and I enjoy playing host.

I am told that some of our parties are considered, by some of our friends, to be the main social event on their calendars. ("I'd kill for an invitation" is how one of them put it.)

What makes them so successful? Let's start at the very beginning.

Theme is different from occasion, which is different from purpose. The purpose of my parties is to bring together people who I like so that we can all have a good time. The occasion could be, say, the celebration of an anniversary. As for the theme, it could be anything that strikes my fancy. Generally, it's an item from history, current events, or pop culture. Decor, refreshments, entertainment, and costumes, if any, all take their cue from the theme.

How do our guests get clued in on this core idea? That's the job of what I call my silent salesman, the party invitations. I'm a firm believer in first impressions (no pun intended), and isn't it from the invitation that people get their initial inkling of what a given party will be like?

The following highlights some of the more memorable parties Harry and I have given since we tied the knot in 1952.

Mitchell's Bar Mitzvah-Summer of 1971

After celebrating our great joy at the Western Wall in Jerusalem, followed by a brunch at the King David Hotel, we made an unforgettable event in New York in order not to leave out all of our friends here. We converted the Riverdale Jewish Center into a courthouse and put pillars of Justice in front of the building. We built up a jury box inside for the children to sit in and we put a big sign in front of it which stated, "Juvenile Jewry." The waiters were dressed like English Judges with white wigs and white gloves (when they walked around people could not help but laugh). Our bartenders were dressed like convicts, in black and white striped outfits. Harry announced that those were our clients whose cases we lost! Everyone who entered received a legal brief and in it were the songs which we sang about our family and profession.

For example we had a song, "Oh What A Beautiful Law Suit." and a song about his Torah portion, Ki Teze, to the tune of "Que Sera, Sera."

> "When he was just a little boy,
> He asked his mother what he should be,
> Should he be a lawyer, or a doctor,
> Or even a great Rebbe?
>
> Ki Teze, Teze, your Bar Mitzvah sedre will be Just follow it carefully, Ki Teze, Teze
> What will be, will be.

When he went out to play some ball
He asked his father, what if he should fall.
Should he go to a doctor, or get first aid,   Here's what his father said:

Ki Teze, Teze,
To a lawyer go out and race,
And see if you can't make a case
Ki Teze, Teze. Ki Teze, Teze.

As usual, all my friends got into the spirit of things and one of them sent me the following poem (which I incorporated into my album):

"How can one properly judge an affair such as yours,
From davening early Saturday, 'till Monday morning petit-fours
Just an ordinary phone call or note would not do,
So I attempt to follow suit, and send this Brief to you.
As for Mitchell at services, surpassed he could not be
But the surprise was the talent of the entire family.
Your Brief was delightful, your skits well rehearsed.

We saw Blech is Beautiful, and learned your talented First.
The convicts and judges knew just what to wear
The scales of justice filled with beautiful flowers
The music and dancing, so 'freylich' for hours. And then when no one could eat anymore, Came candy and toys-a portable store.   So thank

you for going to such a great fuss, The verdict is in: it was truly GORGEOUS!"

Seth's Bar Mitzvah

In May 1975, we celebrated our second son's Bar Mitzvah. Since we had to follow suit with regard to our other son's party, we had somewhat of a dilemma. However, we were able to solve it. We held it at the Starlight Room of the Waldorf Astoria Hotel. The theme was Israel, and we built up the Western Wall and stated on the sign, "This is our Wall of Astoria." Instead of table numbers, we put down cities in Israel and we had waiters dressed as El Al stewardesses take you to your seats. As you entered, we gave each couple a "Bar Mitzvah Magazine." In the middle of the magazine we had put our son's picture with Tallis and Tefilin (phylacteries and prayer shawl).

On the first page of the magazine we listed the names of the guests, under the heading "Cast of Prayers." On the second page we listed the invited children under the heading, "The Answers To Our Prayers."

Of course all the songs we performed were contained therein, such as "He'll Wear Tzitzis That Jingle, Jangle, Jingle" (to the tune of "I've Got Spurs That Jingle, Jangle, Jingle"). Another song, sung by our children in honor of their parents (to the tune of "There is Nothing Like A Dame") was:

> "There is nothing like a claim, nothing in this world. There is nothing you can name, that pays anything like a claim."

Another one of the songs referred to his Bar Mitzvah Torah portion and it went as follows:

> "So remember your Sedre, and don't go astray,
> And do as we do, and follow our way.
> If you learn the law of the land, it will bring money into your hand.   But if Torah learning you pursue, to yourself you'll be true.
> CHORUS: Oh, Seth Barry First, for good deeds you must always thirst,
> Even if you're a doctor or lawyer, they must always come First."

At all the place settings on the tables we put Pledge Cards which stated that each person must pledge that twelve years from now they must use Seth Barry First as their doctor or lawyer.

We're Having an Affair

When our anniversary came around in June of 1985, we sent out the following invitation:

> "We're Still Married, And Having an Affair" It appearing that divorce would be too expensive for Harry, and that Lee and Harry are still blissfully married, it is ORDERED that all of you who are happily married are invited to our party, for the purpose of seeing how many of you have held out together and can still have fun, and would dare to share in an affair.

I then proceeded to announce the secret of a successful marriage with regard to each couple present:

Dr. & Mrs. E.B.-As a doctor he knows how to cure the disease which she got when she started law school. It's called "MAIDS," and she won't survive if she doesn't have one.

Judge P.A. and Dr. D.A.-She's a judge and he's a dentist who deals in bridgework. In fact, he's out playing bridge most nights and we know why their marriage works 'cause he's not home too much.

Mr. & Mrs. H.V.-He's in the diamond business and their marriage works because his wife is a jewel of a person.

Dr. & Mrs. E.F.-He stays married to his wife, unlike Adam in the Garden of Eden when they asked him, 'If you had it to do all over again, would you marry Eve? He said, 'No, I'd like to turn over a new leaf.'

By introducing every couple out loud, everyone gets to know each other.

Statue of Liberty Party

When it was the Centennial celebration of the Statue of Liberty, we used that as a theme of our annual anniversary. "Emigrate to a Party In honor of Miss LEE- PRETTY who is holding the Torch For Handsome Harry." I put my picture into the face of the Statue of Liberty and put Harry's picture into the torch. Underneath, I wrote the following verse:

"So bring us your huddled masses with your cocktail glasses. But none of your poor, Your Gucci's for sure."

I said further, "Please answer in writing for whom or what you are holding the Torch, so that you shall obtain a passport to enter the party. You will be asked to pledge your allegiance to Harry First's home of the brave and land of the fee."

We are fortunate in that we have clever and creative friends who are ready, willing, and able to play along with the themes that we suggest.

Our friend who is elegant and, as you can see, brilliant submitted:

> I thought of the charming, I thought of the wise. I thought of the talented, and one would surmise that surely a glimmer of someone would come, But not even the slightest vision of one.
>
> I thought of the brightest, I thought of the best, I thought of the poetic, but no one I guessed. I thought of the clever, I thought of the true I thought of one's beauty; not even a clue.
>
> How to get such a passport filled me with chagrin. It became such a bother, I nearly gave in.

I was also able to make a series of comments about some of the others who were there:

Judge G. and husband E.G.: He's an attorney, and she's a judge. In this case, he gave up his liberty for justice.

D.r and Mrs. R.H.: She is holding the torch for H., because no one can hold a candle to him.

Dr. & Mrs. K:. He's an ophthalmologist, and holds a torch for his eyeful of a wife, E.

Mr. & Mrs. M.D.: He's a partner in an investment firm, and holds a torch for the bond that ties him to his wife.

Rabbi & Mrs. B.B.: He's the eminent Rabbi who is also known everywhere as 'Lee's Brother.' Actually, he tried to tell us whom he's holding the torch for, but when he phoned Harry's office, Harry, as usual, was running to court."

My brother came up with a terrific idea that I was able to reveal to the world for the first time that day.

"He holds a torch for a new type of answering machine that's designed especially for Harry," I announced. "Instead of answering, the machine hangs up on people. The message it plays is, 'When you hear the tone, please hang up... Can't you see I'm busy?"

This verse from Mr. and Mrs. S.R. was read:

> "We carry a torch for thee,
> Harry and Lee.
> Your fun and games
> fill us with glee.
> We've never known
> a more fun couple;
> They serve us food
> with a knife and a 'gupple' (fork).
> Gorgeous Lee, She stands and winks,
> While Handsome Harry serves us drinks.
> So Sam and I, we both agree,
> We carry the torch for Harry and Lee."

One of the attorneys at the party came up with the following ditty (sung to the tune of "America The Beautiful"):

> "Oh beautiful for spacious CASE,
> That brings in Harry's FEE.

> Oh broken staircase causing falls,
> That brings the dough to Lee.
>
> America, America in TORT may you endure,
> To quench the thirst of Lee B. First, And all of us for sure!"

Then there was the doctor for whom I found a wife and who is happily married until today, and he contributed the following verse:

> "To Handsome and Gorgeous I'm loyal.
> After all, they found me my 'goil.'
> To honor 'Lee Pretty.'
> I've composed this brief ditty,
> -Lauding Legality's beauty, most royal."
>
> G-d's done so wondrously:
> He brought together and kept together
> Handsome Harry and Gorgeous Lee."

First v. First

In 1990, when Trump v. Trump hit all the newspaper headlines, we made a party based on First v. First. Instead of an anti-nuptial agreement, we called it a post- nuptial invitation.

I wrote: "I VANNA HAVE A PARTY TO TRUMP EVERYTHING."

Besides for my gorgeous parties, I always like to stay in touch with all our friends at the time of the Jewish New Year and send out a special New Year's Greeting. According to Jewish tradition, what one does on the first day of the new year is a sample of what will follow. For that reason, we eat honey so that our lives will be sweet during the year. I've sent cards that read:

"Have a healthy and wealthy New Year. Remember money is not everything, but it sure helps you keep in touch with your children!"

Or: "May you live long enough to be a problem to your children.

And: "Remember poverty is inherited. You get it from your children."

CHAPTER 16
I LOVE TO DECORATE

Our Israeli children and their families have visited us here and stayed in our apartment. Though Handsome Harry and I are home alone now, we still need our large quarters for when our kids visit. It happens to be a double apartment, but at the rate they're going, we may soon need a triple.

From the time we were first married, I have always taken a great interest in decorating. At that time, we had only half an apartment-a living room and a bedroom. I met this challenge by turning our living room into three rooms. Along one wall, I had a sink, a stove, and a refrigerator installed. Since I believe that no housekeeper in the world can keep a kitchen immaculate enough to be part of the living room, I wanted that area hidden when not in use. My solution was a blind that dropped from the ceiling and was painted the same color as the adjoining walls. At the side of the kitchen, I placed floor-to-ceiling poles with climbing plants between them that curled around the poles.

In another area of the living room, I made the walls a deeper shade, and created a dining room with credenza, table, and six chairs. Opposite that was the living room with couch, chairs, lamps, and coffee table.

The ultimate compliment came when people asked, "Who's your decorator?" It really made me proud to know that I had done it all on a shoestring, even to painting the walls myself.

After being married four years, we moved to Riverdale in 1956, and we've been in the same apartment ever since. We started with a two bedroom unit with the hope of increasing the size of our family. As it turned out, we managed to house two children and a maid in the second bedroom.

I arranged the furniture with the need for privacy in mind. One end of the room had two cribs with a chest of drawers between them. Closed off by a folding screen was a sleeping-couch.

I really enjoyed finding ways of making use of limited space. In visiting friends with small apartments, I never liked having a baby carriage be the first thing to greet my eyes. To avoid that situation in our place, I found a narrow Swiss-made baby carriage that fit into our entrance closet perfectly.

Incidentally, decorating Harry's office gave me a similar feeling of accomplishment. Here, too, I used a few well-chosen pieces-a desk, a couch, and two chairs.

One special addition eliminated the cluttered look I dislike. Built-in cabinets line an entire wall, and into them go files, books, stationery, and assorted junk - all out of sight for a nice neat look.

With the birth of our third child, it was clear that we had outgrown our quarters. Since moving was much too costly, we had to think of an alternative. Sudden brainstorm! I persuaded the landlord to rent us the adjoining apartment, then proceeded to wall off part of it. By subletting the master bedroom, hallway, and kitchen, I was able to cut our own rental costs considerably.

Now we are left with the living room and dinette. The latter became the maid's room. As for the living room, we transformed it into a dining room plus a bedroom for the two children. Since the area had no closet, I built a concealed one along one wall. That way, the pair of chests, clothing-rod, desk, etc. could become as messy as the kids wanted. Once it was closed off, nothing but a wall showed.

The divider between the children's room and the dining room had another function. Two partial walls tall enough to serve as headboards were topped by beaded crystal "curtains" suspended from the ceiling.

As our children grew, fortunately, so did our income. Eventually, we were able to take over the whole other apartment, and our two sons took over the master bedroom. The second living room became a large formal dining room that seats fourteen.

Now I was stuck with two kitchens, but that proved to be no problem at all. According to kosher laws, we're supposed to keep meat apart from dairy products and use different pots, dishes, and utensils for each. Instead of having to explain all this to my succession of maids, all I now had to say was, "Whatever you see in this kitchen, cook in this kitchen, and whatever you see in the other one, prepare only in there."

I have never missed having a house because our apartment has so many great features. Floor-to-ceiling windows give an airy open feeling rather than a cramped, closed-in one. Another terrific plus is our forty-foot terrace which becomes an all-purpose room six months of the year. Starting with breakfast, we eat all our meals out there. It's also where we entertain and read books. For me, it's more convenient than a backyard or a garden of a house would be since it's literally just a few steps from the kitchen.

First-time visitors say that the apartment depicts me, and I think that's how it should be. Our homes should reflect our tastes, our values, and our personality. I love vibrant colors, and could never be happy in a place with drab tones.

Right now, our tones are white, lilac, and silver. Thinking a rosebush in those colors would make a striking accent piece, I went ahead and fashioned one. I began with a branch that I found in the street, cleaned it off and stuck it into a lovely crystal vase. To steady the branch, I filled the vase with those pretty little stones that they sell for fish tanks. Next, I discovered that Woolworth's had just the right lavender flowers, which I fashioned to the branches with thin picture wire. The last step was painting the branches silver.

Whether it involves a single piece like my lavender rosebush, or a whole apartment, I always find decorating rewarding. Since psychologists keep telling us that our surroundings affect our mood, why not go for the gorgeous and feel good?

CHAPTER 17
I BECOME A JUDGE

What was it like for this wife/mother/ homemaker to put on her working hat? Along with my formal education and legal know-how, I brought love of family, respect for Torah, and flair for humor to work every day. Like everyone else, a judge is the sum of his or her life's experiences.

It was in October of 1975 that Governor Hugh L. Carey appointed me to the position of Workers Compensation Law Judge. At a party in my honor given by some of my male chauvinist friends, one of them had the nerve to announce, "Her court room is ready, the mirrors are up!"

One thing should be said for the Workers Compensation Board. Thousands of workers are injured and legitimately compensated by the insurance carriers pursuant to statute. Workers Compensation Law, as administered by the board, is eminently fair, protecting every worker who is justly injured. Cases are heard speedily and payment must be made without delay or else penalties are imposed.

Another key fact about Workers Compensation Court is we do not engage in adversarial proceedings. Rather than try to do the worker out of his rights, we must see that he gets what he's entitled to. We truly go out of our way to make sure that everything is done in favor of the claimant/worker.

Thus, in civil court, if your name is called and you don't answer, your case is dismissed from the calendar. Not so in Workers Compensation Court. We always wait fifteen minutes before taking any action. If the claimant fails to show up once, the case is adjourned. If he fails to appear a second time, the case is closed. If the claimant should arrive an hour after the case has been closed, we will re-open the case and proceed as if he had come on time. It is to be noted that even if a case is marked closed, the claimant is not denied his rights since all he has to do is write a letter to the Board to re-open the case and ask for a hearing. His/her case is good for eighteen years.

The claimant has other rights. All the actions taken by the judge and all spoken words during the session are recorded by the court stenographer. The claimant has the right to appeal the judge's decision (free of charge) to the Board of Commissioners and then to the regular courts. A case can be brought all the way up to the U.S. Supreme Court.

Claimants get courteous and respectful treatment. We're mindful that they have taken a day off from work and have had to travel to get here. Upon arrival, they are summoned into the court room and seated. We then explain the case, and if they are to receive monetary compensation, we tell them the amount.

Fully half the claimants appear without a lawyer. What, you may wonder, makes the other fifty percent spend part of their reward on legal fees?

There are several possible reasons. First, is the fact that the judge explains the case only once, and some claimants do not understand what is being said. Others feel more secure knowing that there is a lawyer at their side ready to repeat and explain the judge's words.

Sometimes, a lawyer is needed to clarify the nature of the injuries sustained, or of the average weekly wage. (Court decisions are based upon this figure.) A lawyer can also corral all the medical evidence needed from the treating doctors for his client. Finally, should the insurance company decide to contest the accident, the claimant needs a lawyer to properly present his case.

There's another interesting distinction between workers and civil courts. In the latter, the plaintiff must produce his own witnesses. It is always difficult to get a doctor to testify, and when he does, he will want upwards of $2000 for the day. In our courts, the per diem fee for the doctor's testimony is fixed at about $200. What is more, he must agree to appear. Refusing means that he loses his license to treat compensation patients.

In workers' compensation cases, producing witnesses is the responsibility of the insurance company, as is paying the doctor of the claimant. All the claimant has to do is show up and tell his or her own story.

Since trials involving administrative agencies like ours do not entitle the parties to a jury, the judge takes on the dual role of judge and jury.

On the subject of juries, by the way, Handsome Harry had an odd experience. Sometimes he doesn't get to see a particular client for an entire year because there are so many of them. That is why he didn't recognize the one-in-a-million event when it happened.

As usual, names for the potential jurors were picked from the voting rolls. In this instance, Harry's client was actually called for jury duty on the same case where he was the plaintiff! Luckily, someone noticed the identical names and the man lost the opportunity to award himself a fortune.

Now that I was a judge, I became the subject of "judge jokes."

A man goes to a country where the people are cannibals, and he sees a sign that says Butcher Shop. He goes into the store and asks to buy a pound of brains. So the butcher says: " We have doctors' brains for $5, we have lawyers' brains for $5, and we have judges' brains for $50." So the man asks, "How come judges' brains are more expensive?" The butcher answers: "Do you know how many judges we have to kill for a pound of brains?"

Or there is another funny story which is a comment on how the judiciary is perceived. It seems a man went hunting and rented a hunting dog for $5 an hour. The dog's name was Lawyer. The man was very satisfied and when he returned the next day he again rented Lawyer for $5 an hour However, when he returned the following day the man said that he could rent Lawyer for only $1 per hour. The customer was astonished since the dog had run around and retrieved everything. The owner of the store then told him, "Yesterday a man who rented this dog called him Judge by mistake and now all he wants to do is sit on his behind and bark!"

CHAPTER 18
SOME OF MY INTERESTING CASES

I am always astonished at the speed of the cases depicted on TV. The whole trial from start to finish generally takes half an hour, including time off for commercials. In the real world, in the civil and criminal courts, cases take weeks or months to try. At the Workers Compensation Court we hear sixty cases per day, only some of which actually go to trial. We have to allow a quarter hour for each witnesses' testimony and a half hour for that of the doctor.

The usual training period for judges at the Workers Compensation Board is twelve weeks, but because of my excellent trial experience record of over twenty years I was assigned trial calendars after only three weeks. I soon acquired a reputation for narrowing the issues and dispensing with unnecessary testimony. In the law, as in decorating, I am opposed to clutter. By cutting every case down to the bone, I got things moving at a brisker pace. This caused one of the attorneys who wanted the minutes of a particular trial to say, "I'd like to order a copy of the seconds, please."

Before long I was nicknamed "Judge Gorgeous" and my courtroom, Part Nine, became known as "Studio Nine." A disgruntled man who had lost a controverted case over which I had presided was heard to grumble, "Justice is Blond."

And this is the story of how I acquired the name Judge Gorgeous because of the prejudice of men in those days. The first day I presided as a Judge, an Italian man walked in and looked around and asked: "where is the judge?" When in fact he was looking for a male, since at that time there were very few women judges. And when I advised him that it was I who was his judge, he got angry and said: "I don't accept that." So I replied: "why not?" And this was his answer: "because you are too gorgeous" (in those days, women were not allowed to have a brain and be good looking simultaneously). So a lawyer in the court said out loud: "let's just call her Judge Gorgeous!" And I did not mind at all.

My father always said, every person has 3 names in this world: one that he is given by his parents, one that people know him by and finally a name he makes for himself. Ultimately, Judge Gorgeous is the name I made for myself in this world.

I am sometimes made aware that I do not fit most people's image of a judge. Take the case of the nice old man who appeared before me without an attorney. Carefully, I took his testimony, and then took the testimony from his treating doctors. I awarded him a generous compensation. As he was leaving the courtroom, he looked at me and said, "I want to thank you very much for being so nice and all, but I was told that I would be seeing the judge today!"

It's customary for us judges to lunch together at which time we discuss cases and unusual incidents.

When I became supervising judge, I gave lectures on the new laws and regulations. There was always a sizable audience of those who knew I'd include a few new jokes and some Torah thoughts. Because of my extensive trial experience, I presided exclusively over controverted (challenged) cases. It was up to me to decide on medical issues and whether the accident occurred in or out of the course of the claimant's employment (a key factor).

It's hard to believe some of the injuries people tried to present as being work-related. Even harder to believe is the fact that the many funny stories still making the rounds are based on actuality.

For example, a prominent cardiologist testified before me about a client who had a heart attack while at work. "He can only do light work from now on," said the doctor quite seriously. "As for food, he can only eat his wife's cooking. He's not supposed to get excited!"

Psychiatrists who appeared before me often shared jokes about their own profession. One such concerns a man who tells his psychiatrist, "No matter what I do, no one pays attention to me." Without missing a beat the doctor looks up and says, "Next!"

Another is about a patient who complains about his low self-esteem. "You don't have an inferiority complex!" thunders the psychiatrist. "You are inferior!"

And finally there's the famous Feinstein test. A psychiatrist testified that there is a reliable way of determining a person's mental illness or health. As it happened, the judge before whom he was testifying had a son with a long history of mental problems. "Tell me more about this definitive test." he said.

"All right," said the doctor, "Here is the procedure. You dial this Bronx number (which he gave) and ask for Mrs. Feinstein. When she answers, you describe all the patient's symptoms. At this point, you know the patient's condition is serious if she says Oy, is he Meshugah! And that's the Feinstein Sanity Test."

I was a judge for eleven and a half years and I came in contact with all kinds of lawyers (which reminds me of a joke): The question has been asked, "Why are lawyers buried twenty feet deep when they die (instead of just five feet)?" The answer is, "Cause deep down they're good people!"

Or there's the story about the luxury liner that suffered an explosion and sank. Soon after sharks attacked the survivors. As people died left and right one man, a lawyer, remained untouched. When he was later rescued, he was asked. "How come the sharks didn't attack you?" His answer, "Professional courtesy."

I have presided over many cases where seriously injured people have appeared before the Workers Compensation Board and their cases were not controverted by the insurance companies. These claimants have all been fairly paid for their loss of earnings and for their medical expenses.

Somehow, I do not believe that any of those cases would have proved as interesting reading as those I have chosen in this chapter. Besides, they are in keeping with my philosophy that a little lightness can help us better face the serious challenges of life that confront us all.

CHAPTER 19
LONG DISTANCE PARENTING

One of the challenges we must all face from time to time is change. For example, the change in the make-up of our household meant revising the way our meals were prepared.

With the kids grown and out of the house, I no longer needed to hire someone to do the cooking. I bought a programmable oven and found I could put in, say, a frozen roast before leaving for work and have it done upon our return. The microwave enabled me to do even better. Now I could have dinner ready in minutes.

Lately, though, with so many good kosher restaurants in New York City, we seldom eat at home anymore except, of course, for Friday night and Sabbath. Eating out is not only convenient, but also fun. We're always sure to run into people we know, and it's a great chance to catch up on the doings of old friends and new.

Somewhere I came across the question: "Why does G-d want us to keep kosher?" One explanation given was, "In order to keep the Jewish nation together." We saw this to be true in our travels. Whether in Florence or Rome, we always knew what was going on in the Jewish community when in the neighborhood kosher restaurant.

These past few years much of our "dining out" has been in Israel. Having two married children and fourteen grandchildren living there is a powerful drawing card. People often ask us what it is like to be long-distance grandparents. We made up our minds not to let the miles make strangers of us, and have been lucky enough to be able to handle the matter as we really want to.

What we do is fly over every summer and winter for a two or three week stay and then supplement those trips with shorter ones whenever we get lonely for the kids or there's a new baby to welcome.

When Seth phoned one Sunday morning with the news that Eta had just given birth to their first child, I dropped everything and headed for the airport.

I had to make one preliminary stop-Boro Park. Here I shopped up a storm for layette, baby shabbat clothes, a carriage, etc. Where did I do my packing? I had brought along empty luggage and packed on the sidewalk right outside the children's shops I'd been hitting.

Then I rushed to the airport and when the plane landed took a cab straight to the hospital. I got there ten minutes before the end of visiting hours and just after Eta came out of the recovery room. She opened her eyes and there I was. Since her own mother hadn't been able to make it to Israel, my presence was doubly appreciated.

We make it a practice to stay at various hotels, generally spending one week in Jerusalem and then pushing on to another city such as Tel Aviv or Eilat. Our kids and grandchildren have a standing invitation to check in right along with us and they often do.

At the hotel, one of the first things they do is take a gorgeous, hot bath. They luxuriate in the warm bathroom that has loads of towels, creams, lotions, etc. Because they lead such a Spartan life in Israel, it's a special pleasure for me to see my daughter call room service or come down to be served breakfast along with her family. As for the children, they love the change of scenery of hotel lobbies, which can present plenty to see and do in and of themselves.

While I'm off shopping with my daughter and daughter-in-law, Harry will babysit solo in the lobby. Surrounded by eight little ones, he's a combination Pied Piper and kindergarten teacher. Playfully, he bosses the kids around and everyone who enters the hotel instantly befriends him and the whole crew. People can't get over the fact that a big, tough lawyer like H.H. can be such a softie around the kids.

It's funny, sometimes, to hear the grandchildren's impression of us and our visits. Until very recently they wanted to know if being at the hotel meant that they were in America. To them it seemed logical, since it was so different from their usual way of life.

Also, one of them remarked that Harry and I must be very rich since we owned so many beautiful hotels all over Israel. And when someone asked my granddaughter if we are her grandparents, she said, "No. They are much too young."

The fact is that we do act younger and peppier when we're there. Upon arriving, I immediately set up a program of activities we can do together-go to the zoo, see children's plays, etc. We never say we're too tired, because it's for such a short period of time. We have wonderful meals out and have lots of fun.

Once, Harry said to one of his granddaughters: "See that young boy without a yarmulke and tzizit, when you grow up, you won't be able to marry someone like that. He's not a good boy."

Her answer, and she was only five at the time, reflects the Lubavitch teaching she had been exposed to. "Oh yes, oh yes," she said. "He is just as good as you and I... The only thing is his mommy and daddy forgot to teach him what is right... But he's still a good person, and he can learn."

If only all Israeli Orthodox Jews had that credo. Accept your fellow Jews. Don't criticize them; just hope to bring them closer to G-d by setting a good example yourself.

Incidentally, our grandchildren really love the gifts we bring from home, namely lots of clothes for each child. Once Chani, aged four, put on the five dresses I brought her, one on top of the other. She insisted on going to sleep that way. Oh well, girls will be girls!

We'd rather bring clothes than toys for several reasons. First, good toys are easier to obtain there. Second, we like to support the Israeli economy by buying playthings, even though they cost a bit more than they do back home. And third, we have the pleasure of sharing the kids' fun while choosing them. We know they'll continue to enjoy them after we leave and will keep remembering us.

Our trip is not over when we arrive back in the States. The first thing I do is call and take orders for what to bring on our next trip. Then I make a tape recalling all that we had done together. We're told the grandchildren keep playing that tape over and over again as a way of reliving all the fun.

The phone calls and tapes serve an important purpose for Handsome Harry and me as well. They're a way of prolonging the feeling of togetherness with our loved ones until the next visit.

We never dreamed that two of our three children would be living such totally different lifestyles and raising families on the other side of the world from us. But thanks to G-d's gifts of modern science we're able to maintain a close and loving relationship with them all.

CHAPTER 20
COMMENTS ON ISRAEL

Even if we didn't have family living there, Israel and her people would occupy a special place in my mind and in my heart.

In fact, that is what I told the Jerusalem City Counselor at the time when we were brought together by Emunah on one of my recent visits. The idea was for us to discuss political and social issues and to compare the current status of women in our respective countries.

It was amazing how much we had in common, despite the contrast in our appearance. As the reporter put it, "The one is conservatively dressed and coiffed...The other, modishly dressed, with platinum blonde locks tumbling down her shoulders, tottering on three-inch heels, evokes the glitz of Manhattan's cocktail circuit and the affluence and sophistication of New York.[12]

It was interesting to find out that we had both known anti-Semitism in pre-Nazi Europe (she in Austria and I in Switzerland), that we had both studied law and become judges, and that we were both Orthodox. In addition to a fulfilling family life, we each managed to combine our careers with community service (she has chaired with the Israel Council of Women's Organizations, Women's Social Services, and Emunah). Among the greatest sources of joy in both our lives are-surprise, surprise!-our grandchildren.

---

[12] Kind of hard to tell which is which, right?

One of the issues we were asked to address was: What progress has been made in recent years towards advancing the status of women and what areas need improvement?

The City Counselor said that increased childcare facilities have enabled more Israeli women to enter the work force. The number of working mothers doubled from 1970 to 1985. That's good news.

She also deplored the fact that women have made very little political progress-only eight of the 120 Members of the Knesset were women.

On a sidenote, we used to have a Rabbi who, when asked "Do women count for a minyan (or quorum)?" answered, "Women do count, but they don't add up."

I, too, spoke of progress and room for improvement. "When I first began to practice law," I said, "I changed my name from Lea to Lee, in order not to be readily identifiable as a woman. You see, back in those days, a male judge or lawyer would simply tear up or discard a letter from a female lawyer."

"Today we have equal access to professional schools and equal job opportunities. But it's still difficult for a woman to become a partner in a law firm and for the older generation to accept her without bias."

An opinion I expressed was, "The presence of a vital American Jewish community is crucial to Israel's existence, both in terms of political and monetary support. Most Israelis would like us to pack up lock, stock and barrel and move here. But it's not something that most American Jews are about to do. Two of our children live here with their families and we make 'vacation aliyah' earning money abroad and spending it there."

"It is not feasible for everyone to make aliyah. But we can and do support Israel and it never ceases to be the focus of our love and concern."

The Jerusalem City Counselor and I agreed that, despite our disparate views, it is vital to keep the channels of communication open.

By the way, I heard that in Israel the definition of an American Zionist is: "A person who gives money to Israel so that someone else can go to live there."

CHAPTER 21
OUR FOOTHOLD IN ISRAEL

Of late, we have developed an even stronger and more tangible tie with Israel. On October 25, 1989, our family proudly shared a thrilling once-in-a-lifetime experience.

To describe what happened that day, I'll quote the remarks made by my brother the Rabbi.

In his dedication speech, he said, in part, "Names." Our sages long ago taught us that names are not simply descriptive. Prophetically, they also manifest dimension of destiny.

"Almost a century ago, when my father, of blessed memory, was born in a small village in Poland, his parents expressed their love of the Holy Land and their dream for ultimate redemption by naming their child Ben Zion-Son of Zion."

"Who would have dared to dream and to hope that someday this infant would grow up to become a Gadol B'Yisrael; would continue a tradition of eight generations of rabbis before him; would serve in capacities of congregational rabbinic leadership as well as Rosh Yeshiva of Yeshiva and Mesivta Torah Emes; would make a home and name for himself in many lands as he was forced to flee from the horrors of the Holocaust; would finally become one of the outstanding figures of the American rabbinate in Lamdut and P'sak; then, after his death, be accorded the supreme honor of having a synagogue named in his memory built in the land of Zion, in the city of Zion, on the mountain of Zion-the closest spot to the Kotel itself, where Jews from around the world may come together in prayer!"

It is true. In the old Jewish Quarter of Jerusalem, a three-story house of taltish stone now bears a plaque that reads: OHEL BEN ZION Beit Knesset. Inside, on the ground floor, is a shul that was endowed by our family in memory of my father, Rabbi Ben Zion Blech.

The site itself has deep significance. According to the findings of researcher Shabtai Zecharia of Jerusalem, the building has been in Jewish hands (after centuries of being lost to us) since 1886. In that year, Rabbi Moshe Tzadik Danon bought it from an Arab because of its beautiful view of the Temple Mount. Rabbi Danon founded a yeshiva and synagogue on the top floor which had a window directly facing the mount.

In June of 1988, the building was sold to Ateret Cohanim, an organization that works at reclaiming Jewish property within the walled city of Jerusalem.

"Ateret Cohanim recently renovated the ground floor of Beit Danon, and converted it into a Beit Midrash in the name of Rabbi Ben Zion Blech, of blessed memory. The building is thereby serving functions similar to those it served over 100 years ago."

Wherever we go in Israel, we experience a strong feeling of history. It's all around us, but it's particularly intense in our little shul located near Hagai Street, on the street of the Iron Gate leading to the Little Kotel.

The brilliant words of my brother addressing the notables of Jerusalem on the day of the dedication should be noted. He stated: "What is the meaning of the word "Zion" which serves as a connective link with my father, as well as the holiest site on earth? It is fascinating that from the second letter forward it spells the word yavon which is the designation for the Greek world with its glorification of beauty and values seemingly antithetical to Judaism. It is the letter tzadlk, which means righteousness, when placed in front of the word yavon that turns it into Zion. What our sages deduce from this is that our faith does not seek to totally reject the world view which worshipped the holiness of beauty, but rather to transform it into the spiritual awareness of the beauty of holiness. We do not renounce the profane-we sanctify it. We do not abstain from drinking wine; we convert it into holiness by reciting kiddush over it. The Jew does not flee from the impurity of the world and say my kingdom is not of this earth; he accepts the noble responsibility to bring holiness to the world as is.

He concluded by saying, "This synagogue is built of stones which have existed for thousands of years and are still here. How do we say stone in Hebrew? It is EVEN. This word is a combination of two words, av and ben, which means father and son. So, as these stones live on forever, so will the Jewish nation live on forever through father and son."

The building is special not only because of the remarkable man whose name it honors and perpetuates, but also because of the way it straddles the past and the future. As Ohel Ben Zion recreates its role of 100 years ago, it makes us mindful at the same time of the generations-to-be that it will continue to welcome.

CHAPTER 22
MY 50TH WEDDING ANNIVERSARY

I asked my colleague and friend: "How many years have you been married?" She answered me: "Let's see, 5 years to Michael, 6 years to Danny..." I told her: "Maria, you cannot add up all your husbands. It has to be with the same man."

So I planned another big party on June 23, 2003, at the Sutton Place Synagogue, and invited 150 people with the following invitation:

> 50 Years is the Jubilee
> When in Biblical times the slaves went free.
> Our marriage will now reach the JUBILEE
> So come and see if we want to be free,
> Or celebrate the renewal of our romancing
> With a fun CHUPAH Dinner and Dancing.
> And to follow our usual trend
> We have invited each and every
> "GORGEOUS" friend!"

The following is the format of our wedding ceremony: Since the theme was the biblical Jubilee, the first people to walk down the aisle were my grandchildren, blowing the "Shofar" (ram's horn), and they were followed by my husband. Harry was carrying a big sign stating: 'FIFTY YEARS OF SLAVERY IS ENOUGH' and he was in chains, accompanied by my son, Mitchell First. After him 8 Bridesmaids marched down the aisle, carrying a big heart, stating "Love". Next came the Maid of Honor, who had a sign: HERE COMES THE "FIRST" REAL JEW-BE-LEE. The funniest people were the Flower Girls, who were two friends about my age. My grandchildren thought that was very funny and asked: Are they coming down in a wheelchair? One of them threw flowers at all the guests, and the other one came down like a little girl with blonde pigtails and crying and sat down on the floor and would not move. Everyone performed with humor, and then I walked in, and everyone stood up and applauded.

As we stood under the wedding canopy, my brother, Rabbi Benjamin Blech, gave the following speech, which, as everyone agreed, was the funniest wedding speech they ever heard, and here it is:

I HAVE BEEN A RABBI FOR MANY YEARS BUT I HAVE NEVER SEEN A WEDDING LIKE THIS-THIS IS CERTAINLY A 'FIRST'.

50 YEARS TOGETHER. THERE IS A BLESSING WHICH OUR SAGES HAVE CREATED JUST FOR THEM AND LET US ALL SAY IT TOGETHER: 'BLESSED BE THOUGH OH LORD WHO HAS WROUGHT MIRACLES IN OUR DAY (She ozo Nissim LeAvosenu Bayiomim Hohem V'Bezman Hazeh) This wedding will be shown on TV Stations under the heading of SURVIVORS.

THIS IS A REMARKABLE MOMENT, SINCE THEY ARE GOING THROUGH THE WEDDING CEREMONY AGAIN, AND YOU MAY ASK 'WHY'. THE PHYLOSOPHER WAS RIGHT; THOSE WHO FORGET HISTORY ARE CONDEMNED TO REPEAT IT!

THEY WERE MARRIED FIFTY YEARS AGO-FOR BETTER OR FOR WORSE. THEY DID HALF SO FAR-FROM NOW ON IT SHOULD BE FOR BETTER.

THERE IS A QUESTION EVERYONE HAS BEEN ASKING TONIGHT; 'WHY ARE THEY DOING THIS?' IT IS A

COINCIDENCE THAT EXACTLY THE SAME QUESTION WAS ASKED BY MY FATHER & MOTHER FIFTY YEARS AGO.

MY FATHER WAS SHOCKED WHEN MY SISTER CAME HOME ONE DAY FROM COLLEGE AND TOLD MY FATHER THAT SHE HAD MET A YOUNG MAN WHO WAS NOT ORTHODOX, BUT LOOKED LIKE CLARK GABLE, AND THAT SHE WANTED TO MARRY HIM. NOW, MY FATHER, RABBI BENZION BLECH, WHO HAD NEVER BEEN AT A MOVIE IN HIS LIFE, AND WHO I NEVER KNEW WAS FAMILIAR WITH THE AMERICAN ENTERTAINMENT INDUSTRY SAID; 'LET HIM BEGONE WITH THE WIND'

MY FATHER ATTACHED SO MUCH IMPORTANCE TO THEIR WEDDING THAT HE ALWAYS SAID; THE MOSHIACH (MESSIAH) WILL COME BEFORE I'LL LET HER MARRY HARRY. WHEN HE FINALLY ACCEPTED HARRY HE DECLARED IT A HOLYDAY; 'TISHA BAV (a sad day in Jewish History)

YOU ALL KNOW LEE'S PHYLOSOPHY; SHE TOLD MY FATHER THAT 'LOOKS' SHOULD NOT BE ONE OF THE REASONS TO CHOOSE A MATE- IT SHOULD BE THE ONLY REASON!!

THEY HAVE A GREAT DEAL IN COMMON. THERE IS A WORD THAT DEFINES THEIR ESSENCE AND LET US ALL SAY IT TOGETHER. THE WORD IS 'GORGEOUS'. WHEN WE ADD UP THE NUMERICAL VALUE OF THOSE LETTERS IN HEBREW GEMATRIA WE END UP WITH THE NUMBER 613, WHICH IS THE TOTAL NUMBER OF COMMANDMENTS IN THE TORAH FOR US TO KEEP, AND THAT IS WHY WE KNOW THAT THEY ARE BOTH GORGEOUS.

THEY MAY HAVE A FEW PETTY DIFFERENCES, TO WIT, LEE IS NORMAL AND HARRY IS CRAZY. BUT IS THERE ANYONE

IN THIS AUDIENCE, BY A SHOW OF HANDS, WHO IS MARRIED TO A SANE PERSON. (No one raised their hand)

A GREAT TRAGEDY IS WHEN YOU MARRY FOR LOVE, AND THEN YOU FIND OUT HE HAS NO MONEY.

AS YOU KNOW, MARRIAGE IS GRAND, BUT DIVORCE IS A HUNDRED GRAND!

TO HAVE A HAPPY MARRIAGE ALWAYS HOLD YOUR WIFE'S HAND – OTHERWISE SHE'LL GO SHOPPING.

TO HAVE A GOOD MARRIAGE THE KEY WORD IS 'COMMUNICATION'-YOU DON'T TELL HIM ANYTHING, AND HE DOESN'T TELL YOU ANYTHING. DON'T DISCUSS EVERYTHING!

ONCE PER WEEK YOU SHOULD ALWAYS GO OUT, HAVE A NICE DINNER AND RELAX. YOU SHOULD GO ON MONDAY NIGHT, LEE, AND HARRY SHOULD GO ON WEDNESDAY NIGHT.

AT MOST WEDDINGS THE RABBI SPEAKS ABOUT THE FUTURE OF THE COUPLE BUT I WILL NOW SPEAK TO YOU ABOUT THE PAST. THEY WERE MARRIED FIFTY YEARS AGO AND BEFORE THE WEDDING CEREMONY THERE WAS THE 'BEDEKEN' (Covering the Bride with the Veil)

FIFTY YEARS AGO HARRY LOVED LEE SO MUCH THAT HE WANTED TO BUY HER A PRESENT, SOME PERFUME. HE ASKED THE SALESGIRL HOW MUCH DOES CHANEL COST AND SHE SAID ONE HUNDRED DOLLARS. THEN HE SAID NO AND ASKED HER HOW MUCH THE PERFUME PASSION WOULD COST AND SHE SAID FIFTY DOLLARS. THEN HARRY SAID NO, SINCE I WOULD LIKE TO SEE SOMETHING CHEAP. DO YOU KNOW WHAT THE SALESGIRL DID? SHE BROUGHT

HIM A MIRROR!! THIS HAPPENED TO HAVE BEEN THE PERFECT GIFT FOR MY SISTER-SINCE SHE HAS NOT STOPPED LOOKING IN THE MIRROR EVER SINCE. HER HOME IS LIKE THE PALACE OF VERSAILLES-A HALL OF MIRRORS.

NOW I WILL TELL YOU SOMETHING WONDERFUL: HARRY WHO DID NOT KNOW THE MEANING OF TZEDAKAH' (Charity) BEFORE HE MET MY SISTER, BY FATE, AND G-D'S REMARKABLE SENSE OF HUMOR, HARRY IS TODAY THE BIGGEST SUPPORTER OF CHABAD IN ISRAEL (meaning, of course, my Lubavitch grandchildren)

LIFE IS A 3 RING CIRCUS, AND THERE ARE 3 RINGS IN MARRIAGE. FIRST COMES THE ENGAGEMENT RING, AND THEN COMES THE WEDDING RING, AND THEN COMES SUFFERING. FIFTY YEARS AGO HARRY SAID 'HARRY AT MEKUDESHES LEE, AND NOW THE WHOLE WORLD IS SAYING THE SAME THING UNDER THE CHUPAH.

YOU SHOULD ALWAYS HAVE CHILDREN IN A MARRIAGE BECAUSE THE KEY TO EXPERIENCING HAPPINESS IS WHEN THEY MOVE OUT AND GIVE YOU BACK THE KEY.

PEOPLE HAVE DIFFERENT INTERPRETAIONS OF WHAT IT MEANS TO BE RELIGIOUS, AND THEY MIGHT NOT APPRECIATE IT WHEN PEOPLE HAVE HUMOR. THEY DON'T REALIZE THAT G-D HAS A SENSE OF HUMOR. HOW DO WE KNOW THAT? I HAVE SEEN SOME OF THE PEOPLE HE CREATED.

IN JUDAISM THE GREATEST IDEAL IS TO SERVE THE ALMIGHTY WITH 'SIMCHACH' (Joy). THE SAME LETTERS OF THE WORD 'SIMCHAH' CAN BE USED IN THE VERB 'YISMACH', AND WHEN WE TAKE THE LETTERS OF THE

LATTER WORD WE CAN SPELL WITH IT THE WORD 'MOSHIACH.' IT IS A CHASIDIG BELIEF THAT THROUGH JOY WE WILL BRING ABOUT THE COMING OF THE MESSIAH.

WHEN THERE IS A FUNERAL EVERYONE MAKES SURE TO ATTEND, BUT WHEN THERE IS A HAPPY EVENT, THEN WE CAN SOMETIMES MAKE IT AND SOMETIMES WE ARE TOO BUSY. THAT'S WHERE WE ARE FOOLISH. WE SHOULD GRAB THE OPPORTUNITY TO EXPERIENCE JOY AND THAT'S WHY WE ARE ALL HERE TONIGHT TO SHARE THIS JOY WITH LEE AND HARRY.

I AM GOING TO TEACH YOU SOMETHING TONIGHT. YOU KNOW AT EVERY HAPPY OCCASION WE SERVE WINE AND LIQUOR AND SAY 'L'CHAIM.' WHY DON'T WE USE OTHER FOODS, SUCH AS WATER, JUICE, ETC. THE ANSWER IS THAT THESE ARE THE THINGS THAT DIFFER FROM ALL OTHER THINGS, SINCE EVERYTHING IN THE WORLD AGES AND DECAYS WITH AGE, BUT WINE AND LIQUOR IMPROVE WITH AGE, AND THUS MAY ALL OF US IMPROVE WITH AGE, AND SAY 'L'CHAIM' SO THAT ALL OF US WILL BE PRESENT AT THE 75th WEDDING ANNIVERSARY OF LEE & HARRY BECAUSE THESE PEOPLE REALLY KNOW HOW TO THROW A PARTY. MAZEL TOV.

After the ceremony we all proceeded to the Social Hall for a sumptuous dinner and dancing galore, and I must say everyone was in high spirits.

I then took the video of my party and showed it on my cable show so that all my viewers could share in my happiness and have fun. (By the way, the name of my Cable show is "Blonde & Beyond")

CONCLUSION

As must be clear by now, there's a serious side to me, despite my love of and preoccupation with the lighter side of life.

Incidentally, some people might call me shallow because of my constant pursuit of simcha (fun). But, as I see it, having a cheerful mien is a good deed. Going around with a long face all the time, and in effect, telling the world: "Look how sad I am, and how much I am suffering" can be considered an act of conceit. Must everyone share your troubles? As one Rabbi put it "The person who is happy, has already done a good deed."

Furthermore, Jews do not believe in any form of asceticism, self-denial, or self-flagellation. We are told in the Bible that those who don't enjoy this world will have to account to G-d when they pass on to the next one.

I believe that when we wake up in the morning, we ought to thank G-d that we are well and try to appreciate the little things in life. In the words of a well-known comedian, "Here's how it is at my age. I look in the obituary page each morning, and if my name isn't there, I get up!"

As part of our enjoyment of life, Harry and I make a point of following the American practice of going out every Saturday night. I once mentioned this custom to Seth, fully expecting him to ridicule it. Instead, he said, "You're right...After all, the Sabbath is our day of spiritual rest. When the Sabbath Queen leaves us, it's not right to jump back to our worldly concerns at once. We have to accompany her out."

When the kids were at the dating and marriage stage, I often found myself in disagreement with them. One day at work, I told my friend Maria how upset Harry was, and how he wished he could orchestrate our children's lives. "He wants them to be happy," I said, "but he wants to be happy, too." "That's impossible!" she answered. "You know I have a 21-year-old and a 24-year-old, right? Well, in all those years, I have felt like a perfect mother for only one week. "When was that?" I asked. "Last year when my daughter said, 'I'm getting married. He's amazing, he's a doctor, and he's gorgeous.' "Sounds like the answer to your prayers." "You'd think so, right? And the very same day my son showed me his law school report card, with excellent grades." "Terrific! So what went wrong?"

"The very next week my daughter told me they wanted to take more time. I had to cancel all the elaborate wedding plans, then tell both his parents and mine. It was not a pleasant task. The next day my son came home with the announcement that he really didn't want to finish law school or become a lawyer."

Her tale of woe reminded me that we really can't count on the way that things will turn out. Only G-d shapes the master plan. For us to presume to know it too amounts to a negation of G-d. And to think of ourselves as in any way omniscient, would be truly presumptuous. The Bible plainly tells us, "There are things that shall remain hidden from you." As my brother often reminds us, "Don't say. 'Seeing is believing.' Seeing is not believing. You have to believe in things you do not see or, for that matter; even understand."

Another interesting challenge for us is constant change. A metaphor we hear all the time is that we're "traveling on the highway of life." it's a good comparison because of the shifting scenery it implies. "Don't get too excited about anything," it tells us, "because tomorrow may be totally different."

Why did G-d create night and day? Why wasn't it set up for there to be light all the time? One answer is that when light follows darkness, as it does, it brings a new beginning. One can arise each morning with fresh hope. This book includes a number of references to the Bible. That is no accident. I am constantly striving to learn and, as we said earlier, the fact that there is only one Hebrew word (lamed) for both "learn" and "teach" means that it is our duty to share with others what we have learned.

Another of my strong convictions is always to act with love for my fellow man, and to do good deeds, not for any special reward in this world or the next, but only for their own sakes.

We are warned of the danger of excessive indulgence, whether in food, in exercise, etc. The sole exception is that we can never be made to suffer for performing too many good deeds. In fact, the opposite is true: it is said to bring us happiness.

The idea, though, is to let it end there. It is as though I were to say to my child, "Bring me the newspaper, please, and I will give you a quarter." The child then would be good to a parent just for money and would merely be doing a job.

On the other hand, bringing the paper without thought of reward would be showing love for his parent. This, then, is what is required of us in connection with G-d.

When I mentioned my friend's predicament before, it was not to illustrate the uncertainty of life, not to console myself through another's unhappiness.

Looking at those who are less fortunate in order to realize how well off we are, promotes the bad habit of living by comparison. It can happen the other way as well, so it doesn't do to envy those who are fortunate, either.

What then is the solution? To my way of thinking, it can be found in one of my favorite biblical quotations: That person is happy who is happy with his lot. Thus, when I think of my hopes for the future, I keep coming back to that passage. Of course, I would love to be a famous judge, author, or star, but I am perfectly content with the status quo. I think I got this attitude from my father. Every night he would call me. Invariably, he'd open the conversation by asking, "What's new?" When I said, "Nothing much," his answer was always a fervent, "Thank G-d!"

SUMMATION OF JUDGE GORGEOUS TODAY

At age 95, thank G-D, I'm still functioning and making people happy.

I do wonderful Instagrams twice per week with erudition and humor and they go worldwide. You can find me on Instagram @judgegorgeous.

I run a Yiddish club in New York City once per week to tell a Jewish story and a Yiddish joke to uplift everyone's spirits.

Every Sunday night, I invite people to stay at home and join my Zoom meeting to seek a Shidduch. I interview the participants and introduce them to each other.

I also wrote and published another book in 2019, entitled LIFE CAN BE FRAGILE, HANDLE WITH PRAYER. It is available to be purchased on Amazon, authored by LEE FIRST.

To sum it up, everywhere I go, I try to cheer up everybody I meet, and people even ask me for "Bruches" (blessings). I have many "Chassidim" (followers) that cherish me!

SOME OF MY FAVORITE INSTAGRAMS

Have a 'GOOD' New Year

On New Year's Day everyone wishes one another a "Happy New Year." But Jewish people, when it comes to our new year, we don't ever say "Happy New Year." What do we say? "Shana Tova." Have a 'good' year. Now what is the difference between us having a happy year or a good year?

Happiness means selfishness-you should get everything you want, that makes you happy. But having a good year means you should have a meaningful year. While happiness means to take, being good and meaningful means to give. And when you give to the world, the byproduct will be: True happiness.

As a matter of fact, my mother, when she was 98 years old was asked: "How did you do it? How were you happily married to my father for 65 years?" She answered: "To tell you the truth, I did not know I had to be happy."

That's the most clever thing I ever heard. If we don't always think about what makes us happy, we can go on with life. We make ourselves happy by bringing happiness to other people.

Tu B'Shvat

There is a holiday for the Jewish people that is knows as Tu B'Shvat. It is the holiday for the trees and nature, as soon spring will be here, and G-D will revive everything. It's a miracle how nature works, so therefore we celebrate and we eat all kinds of fruits. We say a 'Bracha,' a prayer of thankfulness, for everything we eat, because we must appreciate everything that G-D has given us. And so, we appreciate everything we can do every day. Even when we go to the bathroom, we thank G-D that we can; we say a prayer 'Asher Yatzar.' We continuously thank G-D for everything that He has given us. Therefore, when we have something good, like a good husband, we should always appreciate him.

So when I had my husband, he was so handsome and fabulous, and every day, I did not call him by his name, Harry. I gave him a special name: "Handsome Harry." And if I called him by his real name, do you know what he would say? He said: "What did I do now? Please, don't call me just by name!" I call him gorgeous, wonderful, and that's the kind of marriage we had, and that's what everyone should do-appreciate 'even' your husband.

Purim

"Chag Purim, Chag Purim!" It's time to take off our Coronavirus masks, and put on our Purim masks of joy. We are ordered to be happy on Purim.

Now I will tell you, the hand of G-D was hidden in the whole Megillah (Story of Esther), it doesn't say anything about G-D. But we know that G-D has helped us in a hidden way. That's why we have to wear a mask and a 'polyESTHER' gown, and look gorgeous. And, Queen Esther, has hidden the fact that she was Jewish in order to save the Jewish nation at the time. So we wear masks to commemorate the hiding that has been done. The main thing we should know is that G-D's help is hidden, and we all believe that soon we're all going to be saved from the pandemic we are going through. G-D's hand will be seen once again, as it has always been in the history of the Jews, G-D has always helped us. You may not know, even though we don't see Him, we know we are going to get through this. And that is why when we say Shema Yisrael, we cover our eyes. To show that although we don't see G-D, we still believe in Him and know that He takes care of us.

So what have we been directed to do on Purim? We have to eat, have joy, have a feast, and read the Megillah. The Megillah is part of the history of the Jews, we must read it again and again to know that everything will be alright, and that our future redemption is coming!

A TRIBUTE TO MY FATHER, HARRY FIRST, ON THE OCCASION OF HIS SHELOSHIM

My father passed away on September 2, 2016, at the age of 91. I wanted to share his life story.

He was born in Brooklyn in 1925. His mother died when he was 17. Shortly after his mother's death, he enlisted in the US army. In the summer of 1944, at age 18, he was sent to France and served as a machine gunner. A few months later, his division was overtaken by the Nazis in Alsace-Lorraine and he was captured.

How did he survive in captivity? One of the first things he did was throw away his dog tags, so his captors would not know he was Jewish and give him "special treatment." Because he knew Yiddish, he understood much of what his captors were saying and could even speak some German. But he had to avoid using certain Hebrew words that made their way into Yiddish that might give away his Jewish identity. He made sure to listen more than he spoke.

He remembers that the German guards were very anti-Semitic. Once a German guard showed him a picture of Hitler and said: "Do you know who this is? He is the man who took everything from the Jews and gave it to us." And when President Roosevelt died in April 1945, they came into the barracks shouting that "Rosenfeld" was dead. To them, the U.S. president was a Jew named "Rosenfeld!"

He often had to think fast. When a Nazi guard wondered where he had learned German, he told him that he was a student. The guard got suspicious. "If you are a student," he asked, "Why are you not an officer?" My father says he looked down at the ground as though ashamed and came up with the following response: "Because I drank too much." The guard was satisfied with this answer. (My father later wondered whether the guard might also have had the same problem!)

While in captivity, he bartered his cigarettes for bread and potatoes. He also bartered his milk rations with captured Indian prisoners who had been serving in the British army. They would not eat the meat rations and wanted the milk.

My father initially hid his Jewish identity from his cap- tors and fellow soldiers. But after several months, an American soldier approached him and said the prisoners would probably be dead within three days. What type of burial did he want? My father recalled that the question really jarred him. The thought of a cross over his grave hit him so hard that for the first time he risked his life and admitted he was Jewish. But it turned out the soldier was working for the Germans. My father and the other captives who admitted to being Jewish were then singled out for harsher treatment.

When the war was over, he went to Brooklyn College and Brooklyn Law School on the "GI bill." The government paid for the education of its former soldiers.

He became a lawyer and encouraged my mother Lee to become a lawyer as well. They practiced law together for 20 years. After lawyers begin practicing, many have the urge to become judges. My father encouraged my mother to achieve this goal. In 1975, New York Governor Hugh Carey appointed her as a judge in the Workers Compensation court. She held this position for 12 years. (Her accomplishment was especially impressive since she had come to this country from Switzerland at age 13, not knowing any English.) My father retired from the practice of law in 2005, at the age of 80.

My father was always very optimistic. One of his favorite sayings was "When life gives you a lemon, you should turn it into lemonade." After being a teenager in the army with bullets and death all around him, nothing in any courtroom ever scared him. Also, his ability to think well on his feet, nurtured while in captivity, helped him when he was in court.

One time, my father was trying a case in Staten Island. A statement he made offended the judge, and the judge ordered him put in handcuffs. My father responded by telling the judge he had fought the Nazis as a teenager in World War II and nothing the judge did would scare him. The judge was so impressed that my father had fought the Nazis, he ordered the bailiff to undo the handcuffs and forgave whatever my father had done to offend him.

My parents were among the founding families of the Riverdale Jewish Center. They came to Riverdale in the 1950s, when there was practically nothing there. My parents were also very involved in the founding of S.A.R. I was born in 1958. In the early 1960s, the two dozen of us young Orthodox children in Riverdale needed a school to go to, so my parents helped found the Riverdale Hebrew Day School. In 1970, this small but growing school merged with two other schools: Akiba and Salanter. These schools were located elsewhere in The Bronx, in areas with declining Jewish populations.

One of the committees my father was on was the naming committee. He suggested naming the school "RASHI," an acronym for: Riverdale-Akiba-Salanter Hebrew Institute. But the representatives of the Salanter school insisted that the "S" had to come first, since R. Salanter was a prominent figure, and that school had a longer history and more students than the Akiba and Riverdale schools. That is the in- side story of how S.A.R. got its name.

How did my parents meet? My mother's father was an Orthodox rabbi and educator, Rabbi Benzion Blech. He always wanted my mother to marry someone Orthodox and very learned. But my mother had other ideas. While attending Brooklyn College, she saw my father from afar, while he was working as a librarian in Brooklyn College. He was attending Brooklyn Law School at the time. It was love at first sight for my mother. After she won my father over, came the harder challenge: convincing her father. My father was not Orthodox and never met an Orthodox person before. He did not at all fit her father's image of a son-in-law.

An old friend of my mother's, "Chayele," now advanced in years, recently told one of my sons the following story: My parents had been dating, but Rabbi Blech did not know about it. Chayele came up with an idea. She told my father to sit in the front of the room where Rabbi Blech was giving a shiur. Every time Rabbi Blech finished a thought, my father should nod his head approvingly and mutter: "A gut vort."

My father did this and then after the shiur, as Chayele hoped, Rabbi Blech walked over to one of his talmidim and asked "who is this new illui in the front row? Maybe he's a shidduch for my daughter!"

I am sure that this story is not true! Nevertheless, in retelling this story, I see myself in the role of the ancient Greek historian Herodotus (5th century B.C.E.) In a famous passage (VII,152), he explains that his role is to transmit the ancient stories that are told, even when he does not believe them. Sometimes entertainment value trumps truth!

The true story, as my mother relates in her book, Justice is Blonde, is that her father eventually realized that my mother was not going to marry the learned Torah scholars that he hoped for and was set on marrying the handsome law student she met in the library. Thus, she gradually won her father over to this shidduch with my father, who was willing to become Orthodox. However, the family legend is that Rabbi Blech prohibited everyone in his family from entering a library from that time onward! (I apologize for telling another humorous falsity here!)

One time a friend of my father's warned him that by marrying my mother, he would not be able to eat in restaurants again. He was thrilled with the thought. Having lost his mother at age 17 and having eaten out since then, he was looking forward to a life of home cooking.

My father put his life on the line to fight Hitler. G-d rewarded him with arichat yamim. May his memory be a blessing.

-Mitchell First

My Parents:
Rabbi Ben Zion and
Rebbitzen Gertrude Blech.

Harry proposing on one knee in Brooklyn College.

My parents walking me down the aisle at my wedding in the Gold Manor in Brooklyn in 1952.

Handsome Harry and Gorgeous Lee
at their wedding.

Handsome Harry of the
100th U.S. Infantry Division.

Mitchell's Bar Mitzvah
with head table flanked by Pillars of Justice
and labeled "Juvenile Jewry."

The waiters were
dressed as British judges.

First family celebrates
Seth's Bar Mitzvah
at the Starlight Room of the Waldorf-Astoria.

Seth celebrating his Bar Mitzvah at the Kotel with
Uncle Israel Shor (left) and grandfather
Rabbi Ben Zion Blech (right).

Daughter Shari's wedding to Yossi    Wedding of Seth and Etta First

Wedding of Mitchell and Sharon First

At 25th Wedding Anniversary Celebration: Rabbi Ben Zion Blech and Rebbitzen Gertrude Blech Accompany their daughter down the aisle.

Under the *Chupah*, Lee removes Handsome Harry's handcuffs at the 25th Wedding anniversary Party.

Handsome Harry and Gorgeous Lee on their
40th Wedding Anniversary,
With one of their favorite couples,
Madeline & Stanley Title.

At 50th Wedding Anniversary,
Under the *Chupah*.

> **A NEW BABY**
>
> *is present*
>
> **LEE AND HARRY FIRST**
>
> announce the admission of a new member into the firm of
>
> **FIRST & FIRST, ESQS.,**
>
> To wit: **MITCHELL MARK**
>
> Admitted into the world court on
> **JULY 14, 1958**
>
> Sworn in at 6 lbs. 14 ounces, at the
> Flower Fifth Avenue Hospital
>
> SPECIALIZING in the practice of pleading and loud crying—
> in preparation for trial work.
>
> HEARINGS may be heard daily at the residence
> of the Firsts.

The birth announcement of our first child.

> The firm of **FIRST & FIRST, ESQS.**
> hereby declares its second annual
>
> **Stork Dividend**
>
> to wit: **SHARI JAFFA**
> assessed at: 7 lb. 4 oz.
> delivered on: July 27, 1959
>
> No statement is issued at this time as to when the firm intends to declare a similar dividend-all interested persons will be notified as to further CORPORATE BODY developments.
>
> This acquisition is the result of various maneuvers and MERGERS on behalf of our Growing firm, and will increase the (PAR)ent VALUE of its FIRST CLASS STOCK.

We delivered a "stork" dividend when our daughter, Shari, was born exactly one year after our son, Mitchell.

> **YEARNING STATEMENT**
>
> Due to a favorable Yearning Report, this year the firm of
> **FIRST & FIRST**
> has been able to declare another capital gain distribution (since it took longer than 6 months to acquire)
>
> Although the firm specializes in ACCIDENT CASES, we wish to point out that the within is NOT the result of an ACCIDENT.
>
> The verdict of the Supreme Judge was
> **SETH BARRY FIRST**
> granted at Flower Fifth Avenue Hospital, on May 22, 1962 and judgment has been entered at 7 lb.   oz.
>
> Decision is reserved and the prognosis is guarded as to any future yearnings, and no appeal may be had therefrom without the consent of both parties.

We yearned for another child and instead of an earning statement we issued a yearning statement when our son, Seth, was born. He was our third child.

Family get-together on Riverdale Terrace
Back, L-R: Lee, Harry, Sharon and Mitchell.
Front, L-R: Granddaughter Sima Bella, and Etta First holding daughter Devorah.

Visiting the Swiss Alps

5758 The New Year Stock Certificate

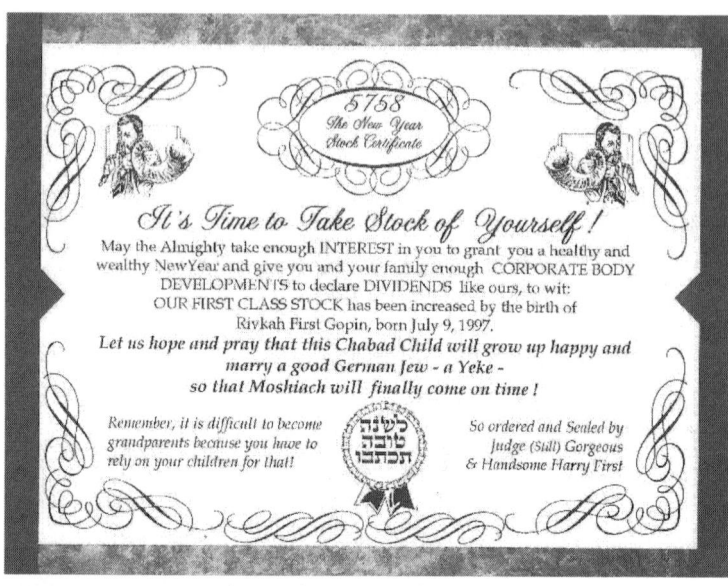

It's Time to Take Stock of Yourself!

May the Almighty take enough INTEREST in you to grant you a healthy and wealthy NewYear and give you and your family enough CORPORATE BODY DEVELOPMENTS to declare DIVIDENDS like ours, to wit:
OUR FIRST CLASS STOCK has been increased by the birth of
Rivkah First Gopin, born July 9, 1997.
Let us hope and pray that this Chabad Child will grow up happy and marry a good German Jew - a Yeke -
so that Moshiach will finally come on time !

Remember, it is difficult to become grandparents because you have to rely on your children for that!

So ordered and Sealed by Judge (Still) Gorgeous & Handsome Harry First

Rosh Hashana Card 1997

Lee First with her new chasidim in the Catskills (2021)
It is the women who have the zechus to bring Mashiach!

Meeting my new Chasidim in the Catskills on Shavuos

Wonder Woman
FOREVER YOUNG

> Today I made a shidduch and I went to a shiur. Then I was in all five boroughs. I took my grandchildren to lunch, then I went to dinner and danced the cha-cha-cha, and I was the star and now I'm looking for a party and to wish you a Shana Tova!

You are invited to a celebration party for the 90TH BIRTHDAY of Judge Gorgeous a.k.a. Lee B. First to be held:
Sunday October 14, 2018
7:00 pm
Sutton Place Synagogue
225 East 51st Street, NYC

Please RSVP to
718-548-6273
judgegorgeous@gmail.com

YOUR PRESENCE IS OUR PRESENT!

My 90th Birthday Invitation

July 23rd marks an important date
Causing many people to celebrate

It's my birthday and I would love to have an "affair"
But because of the corona virus I cannot have anyone there.

Thus I ask you to stay home and zoom in to me
So that all my friends I once again can see

And by our togetherness
uplifted we'll be

With humor, Torah insights and fun.
And to buy a new outfit you don't have to run

Or to find a place to park your car,
Since you can celebrate with us wherever you are.

And since this party does not cost me a cent
I have invited each and every gorgeous friend.

Everyone who comes could tell a joke or say words few
But if you choose to speak everything may
be held against you

So if you want to be heard at this event
Your name beforehand to me should be sent.

So bring your own liquor and cake
So that a LECHAYIM WE CAN MAKE.

JUDGE GORGEOUS
Lee Blech First
NOT 90 YRS, BUT 3 TIMES 30 YRS OLD

My 92nd 'Covid' Birthday Invitation

SWISS MISS

O hear O hear,
Friends from far and near
Again we must celebrate this year
As my 94th Birthday is here!

I am close to G-D as a Swiss Religious Miss
But the entrance to heaven at this time I'd like to miss

So with all of you together humbly I pray
That in this world a little longer I can stay

It's a miracle that at my age I can still write this pun
But when asked to take the steps upstairs and have some fun
I must answer: BOTH THINGS CANNOT BE DONE!

To want to live is a natural drive,
BUT IT'S ONLY WITH GODS BLESSING I will MAKE IT PAST 95

With Love, Judge Gorgeous ♥

My 94th Birthday Announcement

I come to you as princess peach,
so listen to my speech.
Today is Purim and tomorrow it's finished,
but we Jews will never be diminished.
And it's not a chiddish
that tonight we'll make a big Purim kiddish.
We are here today to pray, stay and play.
And as Purim is here,
we will bring you all great cheer.

Love, Judge Gorgeous

Purim Card 2022

Lee First Dressed as "Middos Malka" Purim 2023

Writing the letter ק (100) in the Torah

You're invited to my Zoom birthday party!

July 23 is an important date
Causing many people to celebrate
That all of us are still alive
To watch me reach the age of 95!

On June 13 at 8 pm
You are required at home to be
And Zoom in to celebrate with me
So that all of my friends I can see!

Bring your own liquor and cake
So that a LECHAYIM we can make
There is no need to park your car
You can celebrate wherever you are!

And since this party will not cost me one cent
I have invited each and every gorgeous friend
And let us imitate me and pray by far
That all my friends are as gorgeous
as I think they are

Please do not send me a gift
Just your presence will give me a lift
So come hear words of Torah and jokes you may tell
For G-d said, "Bring SIMCHA to
My world and I will KVELL!"

**Lee Blech First
a.k.a Judge Gorgeous**

June 13 @ 8 pm

Zoom Meeting ID:
409.092.8703
Password: 12341

tinyurl.com/LeeZoom5

Rsvp to judgegorgeous@gmail.com

My 95th and most recent Birthday Invitation

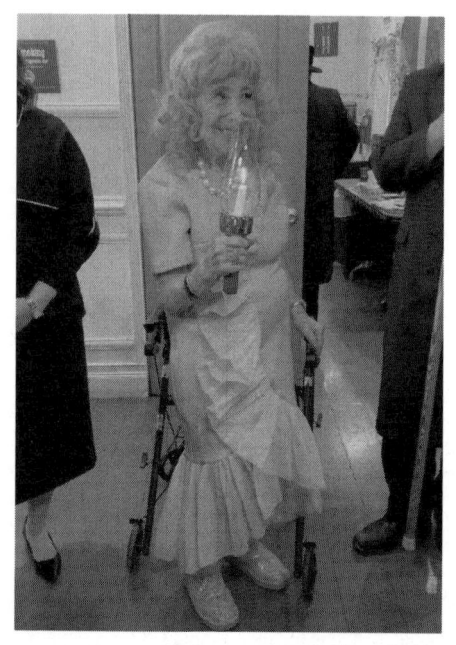

Lee at her Grandson's Chabad Wedding

Judge Gorgeous

Lee Making Tzitzis for the IDF Soldiers

Gorgeous Lee today, age 95

Made in the USA
Columbia, SC
28 August 2024